# MENTORING
## A to Z

# MENTORING
## A to Z

JULIE TODARO

AN IMPRINT OF THE AMERICAN LIBRARY ASSOCIATION

CHICAGO • 2015

**JULIE TODARO** is the dean of library services at Austin Community College in Austin, Texas. She is also a management consultant and frequent workshop presenter. Her research and publications are focused on the twenty-first-century management of nonprofit environments and include best practices in human resources, customer service, and emergency preparedness. Todaro earned her master's degree in library and information science from The University of Texas at Austin and her PhD in library service from Columbia University, New York.

© 2015 by the American Library Association

Extensive effort has gone into ensuring the reliability of the information in this book; however, the publisher makes no warranty, express or implied, with respect to the material contained herein.

ISBN: 978-0-8389-1329-1 (paper)

**Library of Congress Cataloging-in-Publication Data**
Todaro, Julie, 1950–
 Mentoring A to Z / Julie Todaro.
  pages cm
 Includes bibliographical references and index.
 ISBN 978-0-8389-1329-1 (print : alk. paper)  1. Mentoring in library science. I. Title.
 Z668.5.T627 2015
 020.71'55–dc23
                    2015001377

Cover design by Alejandra Diaz. Imagery © Shutterstock, Inc.

Text design and composition by Neuwirth & Associates in the ITC New Baskerville STD and Avenir Next LT Pro typefaces.

♾ This paper meets the requirements of ANSI/NISO Z39.48–1992 (Permanence of Paper).

Printed in the United States of America

19 18 17 16 15                5 4 3 2 1

# CONTENTS

# PREFACE

**WHILE THE CONCEPT** of being a mentor and mentoring others goes back—literally—hundreds of years, mentoring in the business world has come and gone in popularity but has enjoyed a huge resurgence of interest and use in the last decade. The reasons for this are many, and while most would like to believe that increased breadth and depth of usage is due to the value of the mentoring process above all other aspects, the reality is that many use mentorship instead of, as well as alongside, staff development. Mentorship is used as part of or in place of significant orientation and for acculturation of individuals to new or changing programs. In addition, contemporary mentoring programs are used as infrastructures for succession planning to ease transitions and ensure continued policies and processes during times of change. While none of those reasons are bad or inappropriate ones for using mentoring, those interested in implementing either single-mentor relationships or even expansive mentorship programs should study the whys of mentoring, the hows of mentors and mentees, and the benefits as well as the negative aspects of mentoring.

That being said, all employees or members (whether they are mentors, mentees, or neither) in an organization, association, or institution should be familiar with the vision, outcomes, and practice of mentoring as well as the application of mentorship policies and processes. If the concept is vetted and determined to fit the situation, *all* individuals should become knowledgeable about the positive and negative aspects of mentoring as well as what it does do, doesn't do, can do, and won't do. This book attempts to give that information as well as tackle the harder issues such as the big successes *and* the big failures of mentoring, as well as the mistakes and best practices of mentoring.

*Mentoring A to Z* takes a look at the process of mentoring as a successful means of growing and building individuals and organizations, institutions, and associations in virtual and actual environments, in both the long and short term and for both classic job responsibilities and special relationships.

# ACKNOWLEDGMENTS

**M**ANY PROFESSIONALS COMMITTED to the concept of mentoring feel that one can't fully write about, present on, or design a mentoring program; appreciate the process of mentoring; or even mentor themselves without having had their own mentor at some time in their career. And, although I don't think it's a *requirement* to have had a mentor, the experience is richer if one has had the successful, positive relationship of the mentor and mentee.

For me, the story goes back many years and includes educators and adult friends from elementary school through my graduate programs. Within work environments, I don't think I've had mentors, but rather a few wonderful bosses who served in the roles of good leaders and good managers. So . . . when acknowledging mentors, my first mentor relationships were with Ruth Isley, Kay Franklin, and Annie Robinson. From them I learned sound educational practices that put students first, focus on content, and emphasize a commitment to creativity, and the importance of applying creativity to the driest and most businesslike environments.

# INTRODUCTION

**W**ORK, ACTIVITIES, AND functions at "work," work in associations and work for other purposes (church, hobbies, and so on) consume much of our time. In fact, when the number of hours we spend "working" in all of these other areas is added up, we spend more time with others outside our family or friends "at work" than we do *with* our family and friends. It is critical, therefore, to explore, design, build, and even perfect these relationships within these other environments and areas in order to have the best possible experiences.

One successful process used in designing and building relationships is the process of identifying activities and contacts outside the normal management and leadership structures that can lead to successful relationships and thus result in enhanced work and expanded commitment to the organization. This process—"mentorship"—is realized through a variety of approaches.

This book attempts to cover the widest variety and broadest of definitions of these approaches, including the classic mentor techniques and processes individuals and groups today use to develop interest and talent in others. These techniques and processes used for mentoring teach management competencies for enhancing or expanding work relationships; developing mentees to build organizations by fostering leadership skills and abilities; and using mentor practices to increase positive work culture as well as knowledge bases for all employees to excel at work. Mentoring also helps mentees to move into higher-level functional or discipline-specific or management positions. In addition, using the concepts of mentoring in organizations is designed to not only increase retention of employees but also to sustain members through encouraging their becoming committed, active association or organization members and member leaders.

Although some mentorship content techniques and processes outlined in the book aren't new, they are presented in expanded ways (case methods, best practices, critical questions to challenge suppositions, and checklists). These techniques and processes provide newer approaches to designing both virtual and in-person mentorship programs; choosing and educating mentors; critical elements of mentorship curriculum; and choosing, educating, and "growing" mentees. Choosing what's right for anyone or any one group includes the review of all techniques and processes, the needs assessment of a workplace or group, and a match of identified needs with appropriate mentoring techniques and processes.

The chapters in this book have both general information and information by type and size of library, and each chapter includes one or more techniques used to illustrate or display content such as a critical question and answer, a case or scenario, or a grid or checklist that can be used for assessment and evaluation.

The content in chapters includes a mentorship overview and definitions; job descriptions with roles and responsibilities; mentor and mentee styles and profiles, with examples including unique aspects such as gender, age, culture, race, ethnicity, and classic aspects of mentor and mentee relationships; twenty-first-century aspects of mentor and mentee relationships; benefits and liabilities of relationships; curricula for mentors and mentees' orientation and training; best practices; and bad news of mentorship mistakes, pitfalls, and hazards. In addition, the book's appendixes include expanded content for internal assessment, examples of programs with both internal and external mentors and mentees, special project approaches, mentor and mentee evaluations, and recommended communication plans.

# WHAT'S IN A NAME?

**F**OR MANY PEOPLE and projects, names are everything. What something is called or identified as can project fame and fortune, indicate levels of importance, or at the very least, status; drive or imply costs; "brand" a project or environment; represent time; identify goals or outcomes; and illustrate worth or value. So, while seemingly unimportant, the identification of mentoring, mentors, and mentees needs to be thoughtfully considered. Obviously, many names are derived from what mentorship in general is, and although twenty-first-century mentorship is the focus of this book, background information on mentorship includes the following.

- There are more formal mentoring programs in academic institutions, and therefore in more libraries in academic institutions. Many terms, therefore, are derived from educational settings.
- Many associations have mentor programs to advance member involvement in and commitment to the association—primarily with a focus on leadership and leadership activities to grow organizational leaders. Leadership content is often used in defining not only mentor terminology, but the general curriculum for mentors and mentees in all programs.

This applies especially to mentors, because their primary responsibility is to lead others.

- A number of mentoring programs exist—both informal and formal—for other types of librarians and library workers, including those in K–12 schools, special libraries, and public libraries. Many of these mentoring programs, however, reside in the associations or organizations that serve or support these environments due to the size of the institution, the number of staff, and the lack of critical mass of people available not only to plan but also to mentor.

- A larger number of short-term mentor possibilities with some longer-term mentoring processes exist in mentorship relationships today. Many identifiers are for time lines and timeliness, because time can often drive mentoring relationships.

- Mentoring processes to complement education programs represent a growing number of mentorship opportunities in both practice and in educational settings. These use faculty in teaching roles and include typically an educational offering (one day, one week, and so on) with a cohort of learners in mentorship roles and continuing education activity. The terminology for many mentor programs characterized by these activities often includes educational terms and designates not only cohorts but time lines for following up on teaching and learning.

- Many newer mentorship programs have been designed to provide online-only graduate library programs opportunities for online-only students. The terminology for online mentor programs will typically use terms to illustrate the digital or virtual nature of the program and specifically program communication.

- Many more mentorship programs and processes exist for librarians, managers, administrators, and leaders rather than for support staff, non-librarians, or board or stakeholder group members.

- Mentoring programs substituting for processes libraries cannot fund or fully fund such as staff development and training and professional development for individuals are often wrapped into mentorship goals and outcomes. Many organizations use the terms of activities they can't afford as names or subtitles under mentorship program articulation.

## • CASE METHOD •

### "BUT WHAT ABOUT ME?"

Although Frankie participated in the focus groups and initial design phase of the library's mentorship program, she was surprised at how she felt when the mentee's name was announced and the roles and responsibilities of both the mentee and Frankie, the mentor, were outlined. As she assessed her calendar and her department's time plan with the mentee, she wondered at how this position would benefit her and her area—outreach. For general guidance, but also specific answers to her questions, she decided to e-mail her manager and ask for a meeting about "integrating the proposed mentee training" into her already busy and overbooked schedule. She knew she had to participate in orienting new mentees; however, she was wondering how her time spent would benefit her busy department.

### Case Steps/Exploration

In using case method, readers are asked to repeat some steps after assessing what they have read. Readers then illustrate that assessment by marking text to guide case exploration of content.

1. Read the mentorship assignment, or case, thoroughly without underlining or noting case elements. Take no immediate position or role. Then, during the second reading, note elements of the case by underlining or circling case individuals or "characters," case facts as stated, case suppositions, and implied as well as clearly stated issues and actual, perceived, or possible problems.

## "BUT WHAT ABOUT ME?"

Although Frankie participated in the focus groups and initial design phase of the library's mentorship program, she was surprised at how she felt when the mentee's name was announced and the roles and responsibilities of both the mentee and Frankie, the mentor, were outlined. As she assessed her calendar and her department's time plan with the mentee, she wondered at how this position would benefit her and her area—outreach. For general guidance, but also specific answers to her questions, she decided to e-mail her manager and ask for a meeting about "integrating the proposed mentee training" into her already busy and overbooked schedule. She knew she had to participate in orienting new mentees; however, she was wondering how her time spent would benefit her busy department.

2. Prepare lists of the important or relevant facts and statements in the situation.
   * The institution has a mentor program.
   * The design of the program included input from existing staff members—specifically through providing feedback in focus groups.
   * The primary person identified in the case—Frankie—participated in at least one focus group.
   * Frankie appears to be surprised by feelings that have come up upon announcement of the mentor chosen and by the roles and responsibilities identified in the announcement.
   * Frankie is questioning how the mentor program—but specifically the mentee—benefits her department—Outreach.
   * Frankie has questions about the mentor program and how it will integrate into her roles and responsibilities. Specifically, Frankie is seeking answers to how she will manage to train someone when she doesn't have time and when mentor training doesn't appear to add value or opportunities to her department.

3. List the characters or "players" in the situation, and—if possible—list them in relevant categories such as those directly involved, those indirectly involved, and those affected by the situation. Other categories or descriptors for characters can be: decision makers, primary vs. secondary characters in the case, and so on.

   - Frankie—primary
   - The mentee—primary
   - The person who will answer Frankie's questions—primary
   - The head of the mentor program—primary
   - Frankie's boss—secondary
   - Other future mentees—secondary
   - Other future mentors (short and long term in the process)—secondary
   - Others in the organization with similar issues regarding mentees and mentor processes—secondary

4. Review the underlined, marked case elements and list the primary or most important issues, elements, and problems in the case/situation.

   - **Issue/Problem:** Frankie is questioning how the mentor program, and specifically the mentee, benefits her department—Outreach.
   - **Fact:** The primary person identified in the case—Frankie—participated in at least one focus group *but* . . .
   - Frankie appears to be surprised by feelings that have come up upon announcement of the mentor chosen and by the roles and responsibilities identified in the announcement.
   - **Issue/Problem:** Frankie has questions about the mentor program and how it will integrate into her roles and responsibilities. Specifically, Frankie is seeking answers to how she will manage to train someone when she doesn't have time and when mentor training doesn't appear to add to her department.

5. Prioritize the most important and least important issues or problems in the situation. At this point in case review, the

time lines indicated by the case should be taken into consideration; however, other aspects of the case may contribute significantly toward prioritizing case elements. Other ways to prioritize could include now vs. later; immediate vs. can wait, and so on.

## Can Wait

"Can wait" elements are important, but should be considered at a different time. For example, the manager of the mentor program should question general program information distributed to the managers as well as information and discussions in the focus groups as this content should introduce and explain *how* managers are involved and what the benefits are to their departments immediately. No one should have left a focus group confused and while the confusion should be handled first (see the "Immediate" list), future steps should include a review of general and focus group content.

- The institution has a mentor program.
- The design of the program included input from existing staff members—specifically through providing feedback in focus groups.
- The primary person identified in the case—Frankie—participated in at least one focus group.
- Frankie appears to be surprised by feelings that have come up upon announcement of the mentor chosen and by the roles and responsibilities identified in the announcement.

## Immediate

- Frankie is questioning how the mentor program—but specifically the mentee—benefits her department—Outreach.
- Frankie has questions about the mentor program and how it will integrate into her roles and responsibilities. Specifically, Frankie is seeking answers to how she will manage to train someone when she doesn't have time and when mentor training doesn't appear to add value or opportunities to her department.

6. After review and discussion of the prioritized situation content, and given the players, elements of the organization, list "what can be done."
    - Frankie needs to ask for clarification on the mentor program and on mentee roles and responsibilities.
    - The administration (and those who manage the mentor program) needs to clarify and communicate the value of the mentor program for Frankie's department.
    - Frankie needs to find time to work with the mentee in accordance with the mentor program.

7. After review and discussion of the prioritized situation content, and given the players, elements of the organization, and so on . . . list "what can't be done."
    - Frankie's boss can't ignore Frankie's concerns and questions.
    - The administration (or those who manage the mentor program) can't ignore Frankie's concerns and questions.
    - The administration must not ignore potential problems of a poorly articulated or explained mentor program.
    - Choose the best one or two solutions given what data is available, and what is missing.
    - Frankie's boss should answer the questions for Frankie and clarify benefits to Frankie's satisfaction but also inform the mentor program manager (and the administration) that program elements may be unclear.
    - Because the program is not clear to someone who participated in the design of the program, mentor program management must assess communication surrounding the program and–if appropriate–revise, but certainly redistribute, program information.
    - Even though it isn't clear whether or not others in the organization are confused about the mentor program, program processes and values as well as *all* employee roles and responsibilities in the program must be clearly communicated.

8. Speculate on the outcome(s) and impact if the solutions are used and put into effect.
   - Frankie's mentee has a successful mentee experience with Frankie and in Frankie's department.
   - Frankie and Frankie's department have a successful mentor and mentee experience.
   - The mentor program is revised—and in particular, the program's value for the entire organization is clearly communicated throughout the organization.

9. Build in an evaluation mechanism.
   - Although the value of a program for a mentee should be easy to assess, evaluating perception and value for the organization as a whole is challenging. Mentor program managers must assess not only mentee success but also conduct assessments of the organization before, during, and after mentor activities. Assessment of perception and value is achieved through evaluating focus groups and overall participant perceptions through pre- and post-focus group interviews with potential mentors; pre, during, and post surveys of departmental employee and mentee perceptions; department head perceptions; mentee work products (such as quality, timeliness, outcomes met); and overall employee attitudes toward the program.

# WHAT'S IN A NAME?

## WHAT DO WE CALL THESE MENTOR AND MENTEE INDIVIDUALS AND RELATIONSHIPS?

Although the majority of organizations identify mentor and mentee relationships as "mentor" experiences, other names can be chosen for the program, process, or individuals. Alternative names or titles can be chosen to define relationships in general and for relationships that—for example—might be less formal than formal or short term vs. long term. A list of names often used instead of "mentor" includes but isn't limited to coach, guru, guide, advisor, or teacher. Program and process identifications vary greatly as well and include some typical and some not-so-typical names:

- The Mentoring (or Mentorship) Program
- Mentor Processes
- Mentor/Mentee Programs
- The Buddy Program (not a common term, but it is often used for first day, first week orientation or first month with orientation and initial assistance only or mentoring as a short term activity)
- The Protégé Program
- The Leadership Program
- The Sherpa Experience: First-Year Guides for New Professionals
- The New X (employee, library worker, and so on)
- The Junior X (employee, library worker, and so on)
- The New-Comer Program
- The Internship Program
- Employee/Worker Sponsorships
- The Career Development Program
- First-Year Advocates
- The Coaching Program (Often not considered mentoring per se, but focuses on specific improvement of job skills, project completion, and performance change)

- Advising/Advisor or Counselor/Counseling (often not considered mentoring per se, but focuses more on individual issues and on individual, sometimes one-shot, situations or decisions that need to be made related to work responsibilities or relationships)
- Resource Coach (not often found in mentorship programs, but if "resource" is used referring to a person as a "resource," it needs one or more descriptors such as Coach or Advisor or New Employee Resource Guide)

Other names or titles include: First Year Navigator, Association New Member Sage, and Teacher/Guide.

And for entities that want to identify *who* might assist categories of employees or members to not necessarily form a longstanding relationship but instead provide access to someone who is looking for answers at the point of need . . . or for one counseling session or one answer, examples include:

- *Resident Expert.* Rather than one specific mentor and mentee relationship, this title focuses more on the "mentor" role available for anyone in the organization who possesses an in-depth knowledge of functions, including the expert or "go to" guru, expert, or process owner.
- *Minute Mentor.* For those who are new or changing positions or taking on a new project [project management, a committee chair, team leadership, special event, program planning or their "first summer club" or a first instruction section with a new population] and might want one "advisory" session with someone who is *not* their supervisor.

Mentoring programs also seek terminology to identify those individuals within the process. That is, if organizations employ a variety of models or relationships, titles or naming of the relationships assist in the identification of levels of programs or types of relationships. Terms include:

- *Matches.* Matches may refer to two people or to a small group such as a mentor placed with one to three mentees.

Descriptors added to terms such as "first year" or "new employee" or "youth services" serve to further identify match goals or outcomes.

- *Pairs.* Pairs refers to two individuals, including a mentor and mentee, but also larger programs who include single mentors grouped with one, two, or three mentees, and often add peer groups—or two mentees as pairs—to enhance communication and active learning activities. An additional term used is "peer" itself grouped with a status such as "peer mentees."
- *Duos.* Duos, like pairs, refer to two people working together in a mentorship program.

Other multiple terms may be used if the program is multilayered, that is, a combination of individuals who might be identified as the primary focus of short-term vs. long-term relationships (example: mentors might be matched with an individual for a year vs. coaches who might offer support for individuals in short-term activities or in project management). Other related activities such as an organization's "leadership program" are designed to educate and inform; however, this term is more often used for larger groups of individuals who have the opportunity to experience leadership roles and responsibilities.

While organizations tend to choose similar definitions for the mentor process, definitions should be carefully vetted to match the organization. That is, during the design phase of the process, the employees (mentors, mentees, or neither) should be assessed for their perceptions of the roles and responsibilities of all involved in a mentor process. Additional mentoring/mentorship definitions that include length of relationship, modes and methods of communication for the process, as well as potential needs met and defined benefits include:

- Mentoring is a long-term relationship that meets a *development need*, helps develop full potential, and benefits all partners: mentor, mentee, and the organization. –SUZANNE FAURE[1]
- Mentoring is a protected relationship in which learning and experimentation can occur, potential skills can be devel-

oped, and in which *results can be measured in terms of competencies gained.* –AUDREY COLLIN[2]

- The purpose of mentoring is always to help the mentee to *change something*—to improve their performance, to develop their leadership qualities, to develop their partnership skills, to realize their vision. –MIKE TURNER[3]
- Mentoring involves primarily *listening with empathy*, sharing experience (usually mutually), professional friendship, developing insight through reflection, being a sounding board, encouraging. –DAVID CLUTTERBUCK[4]
- Mentoring has been proven to be an important relationship in helping individuals *develop their careers and professional identities.* –AMERICAN LIBRARY ASSOCIATION: ALA CONNECT[5]

The broader view of mentoring or mentorship programs sorts programs into categories; however, some categories overlap with aspects of others, and some use category terminology synonymously.

- *Informal mentoring.* Relationships are formed in the absence of an articulated process. The relationship is created spontaneously and maintained informally by the pair. Processes are often more short term than long term and have an infrastructure, with the appropriate length of the shorter-term informal processes being for the life of a project or activity.
- *Formal mentoring/long-term mentoring.* An articulated process is in place and the relationship is facilitated and supported by the organization, institution, or group.
- *Short-term or situational mentoring.* An articulated process is in place but relationships are shorter and are designed for projects or activities rather than longer relationships for extensive acquisition of knowledge.
- *Minute or flash mentoring.* Like the title indicates, minute mentoring illustrates the shortest-term connection for the mentee to get answers to questions from, typically, a process owner or expert in the organization.
- *Facilitated or team mentoring.* Mentoring processes are articulated within the workplace, but the program involves a wider variety of individuals or groups serving as mentors

and resident experts or minute mentors and facilitators. The program includes formal and informal work together to not only guide others but to get questions answered and provide opportunities for shared expertise.

- *Group mentoring.* Departments, groups, or multiple mentors or one mentor and multiple mentees are involved in the experience (which can also refer to the number of mentors that are involved in the mentor process but are involved in different activities).
- *Co-mentoring.* Two specific mentors are specifically matched based on expertise or competencies to mentor one or more individuals in the activity, and the mentoring can be either long or short term.
- *Peer mentoring.* A support relationship is formed between two individuals within the job, position, department, or employee cohort, such as new employees, for the purposes of shared experiences and shared learning or problem solving exclusive of goals, evaluation, or hierarchy.
- *Virtual, digital, or e-mentoring.* The mentoring program and process is carried out online or through online environments for whatever reason.
- *Hybrid e-mentoring.* The mentoring program and process exists with an in-person as well as a significant online, virtual presence.
- *Supervisory mentoring.* When a mentee seeks to gain management experience but cannot be mentored by their supervisor, he or she seeks a relationship with another manager or supervisor.
- *Reverse mentoring.* Also referred to as mentoring "up," this is flipping or upside-down mentoring in which a younger or newer mentor for a more senior person is sought when the more senior person desires a specific skill set—such as technology.

## IS IT FAIR?

Once nomenclature is decided upon, however, the questions aren't all answered but instead are just beginning. And although mentoring is highly recommended for many, if not most environments, many questions are not easily answered. The mentor question everyone *should* ask and answer first for their environment and the sake of the employees and workers is: Are we playing favorites?

## • SCENARIO •

We would like to mentor him, but if we identify him as a mentee and someone as his mentor, won't all of the other employees think he is a favorite or that he has been or will be given preferential treatment?

Even if an organization clearly articulates a mentor program that includes involving others in the design and process—which is highly likely—the process of mentoring someone does evoke perceptions of "favoritism" and "preferential treatment." Managing these issues therefore demands:

- immediate rollout of program goals and outcomes to all in the organization;
- directly addressing possible perceptions, rumors, and aspects of the process that *do* include additional attention but not favoritism—by the very nature of the program;
- careful definition of terms to include roles and responsibilities of mentors and mentees;
- transparent delivery of program aspects;
- involvement of a variety of employees and members of the organization either directly or indirectly involved with the mentorship program, the mentor, or the mentee;
- involvement of those employees and members of the organization who are *not*—either directly or indirectly—involved with the mentorship program, the mentor, or the mentee;
- clear communication regarding the mentee's position and opportunities for future positions; and
- application processes that include competition rather than appointment processes without competition.

In addition, the reality is that extra attention, reward, and recognition should be presented in the most positive way, and managers should consider:

- integrating broader recognition of and attention paid to employees in general;
- increasing program components to include one-shot, shorter-term, or project approaches to mentoring employees who are either not eligible or not chosen for longer-term, full-blown mentorship opportunities; and
- expanding learning and growth opportunities through individual, small group, or large group training or development.

## WHY IT MATTERS HOW INDIVIDUALS AND RELATIONSHIPS ARE IDENTIFIED

Choosing terms specific to a program or a relationship is not a casual decision nor one that should be made lightly. Picking one identifier over another should be based on a variety of elements including:

- what definition most closely aligns with the process;
- what the umbrella organization uses to define the process;
- what elements of the title might match the program or process such as "new" or "first year";
- what terms might be more universally recognizable by those involved; and
- any terms that trigger support (financial or otherwise) for the process.

For the purposes of this book, we will use the identifiers of "mentor" and "mentee." The reality of the mentoring program and process is, however, that the more varied the program is and the more diverse the relationships identified in one program or type of relationship are, the greater are the variety of terms that should be employed.

## WHAT A MENTOR IS AND WHAT A MENTOR DOES

Like any other process within organizations, institutions, or associations, definitions of mentors vary. Just as the definitions or categories of programs must be chosen carefully, mentor definitions should be carefully vetted against the needs and benefits of the organization, institution, or association. Mentor definitions include:

- A mentor is "an accomplished and experienced performer who takes a special, personal interest in helping to guide and develop a junior or more inexperienced person." –STEPHEN GIBB[6]

- "A mentor should have the qualities of experience, perspective, and distance, challenging the mentee and using candor to force reexamination and reprioritization without being a crutch." –CHRISTOPHER CONWAY[7]

- "A mentor facilitates personal and professional growth in an individual by sharing the knowledge and insights that have been learned through the years. The desire to want to share these 'life experiences' is characteristic of a successful mentor." –ARIZONA NATIONAL GUARD[8]

- "A mentor is a more experienced individual willing to share knowledge with someone less experienced in a relationship of mutual trust." –DAVID CLUTTERBUCK[9]

- A mentor is "a trusted counselor or guide. Normally a senior person to the associate. A mentor is a counselor, coach, motivator, and role model. A mentor is a person who has a sincere desire to enhance the success of others. A person who volunteers time to help the associate." –AIR NATIONAL GUARD USA[10]

- "A mentor is someone who can patiently assist with someone's growth and development in a given area. This assistance can come in the form of guidance, teaching, imparting of wisdom and experience." –CHICAGO COMPUTER SOCIETY[11]

- "A great mentor has a knack for making us think we are better than we think we are. They force us to have a good opinion of ourselves, let us know they believe in us. They make us get more out of ourselves, and once we learn how good we really are, we never settle for anything less than our very best." –THE PROMETHEUS FOUNDATION, ANDREW GIBBONS[12]

- "A mentor is someone who has experience-based wisdom and who is willing to spend time on issues related to the development of your career. This person's sole focus is you as the mentee. They do not judge you but work in your best interests and as a guide on the side, not a sage on the stage. Mentors give their time and experience with no expectation of a return of any kind." –AMERICAN LIBRARY ASSOCIATION: ALA CONNECT[13]

- "Buddies help show the new employee the ropes. They share their knowledge and work experiences in a friendly, informal way. They make sure that the new employee knows he/she can contact them any time. Buddies help reinforce a positive work environment and an appreciative organizational culture." –WEBJUNCTION ILLINOIS[14]

- "A mentor is an experienced and trusted advisor. Within the context of a career, a mentor is an experienced person who provides guidance and support to a developing professional." –MINNESOTA LIBRARY ASSOCIATION[15]

The mentoring or mentorship process provides opportunities for those involved on multiple levels to:

- become better oriented and acculturated to an organization, institution, or group;
- find assistance for learning new roles and responsibilities within standard structures of the organization or managerial infrastructure;
- find assistance (exclusive to mentee supervisors) for enhanced learning opportunities of primary and secondary roles and responsibilities outside the standard organizational or managerial infrastructure;
- experience roles and responsibilities outside typical or expected position roles and responsibilities;
- integrate or maximize organizational and association involvement or membership;
- provide opportunities for leadership experience exclusive of position roles and responsibilities;
- provide opportunities for leadership experience inclusive of position roles and responsibilities; and
- reenergize support through discussions on challenging situations.

The mentor can provide opportunities for sponsorship for references and nominations for activities, service appointments, and other positions within or external to the organization; provide visibility through their work and professional networks; provide referrals functions to others who can solve problems or answer questions; provide politically sensitive information, direction, and advice for aspects of organizational politics; and identify challenging work opportunities. Other opportunities of value to mentees include role modeling; support for unique issues; "cheerleading" or positive inspiration for difficult times; advising for shared discussions of a sensitive nature, and if appropriate, of a personal nature; and networking for like-minded relationships such as friendships.

Effective mentors share a number of characteristics that include:

- possesses and exhibits expertise in their profession;
- adheres to high standards;
- keeps current and forward-looking and is on the "cutting edge";
- recognizes and encourages talent in others;
- possesses a broad understanding of the profession;
- is committed to the profession and any unique areas within the profession for which they are responsible;
- provides exemplary service within the profession both internal and external to their organization;
- possesses and exhibits leadership competencies;
- possesses and exhibits values of the profession;
- has demonstrated achievement or has excelled at their work; and
- excels at communication in a variety of settings and through different modes and methods.

In addition, mentors typically have good interpersonal skills, the desire to teach or lead others, can find the time to mentor, are realists, are versed in some—if not all aspects—of career development, and are energized by giving back and recognizing others' successes.

## WHAT A MENTOR ISN'T AND WHAT A MENTOR DOESN'T DO

Although the goal of the mentor is to follow the organization's mentorship program and processes, and the program should clearly spell out what should happen, a useful exercise is to create a list of "what the mentor isn't" or even—more specifically—what the mentor doesn't do. Examples include:

- Although the mentor/mentee relationship could begin as a friendship or end up as a friendship, the specific mentorship process isn't a friendship. The attributes that contribute to a successful friendship, however, can be used in the mentorship process, including listening and responding, providing support, and offering opinions and critiques.
- A mentor does not serve as the mentee's "guaranteed path to promotion" in the organization, and great care should be taken to communicate that or—at the very least—the absence of guarantees.
- The mentor can weigh in on mentee performance issues with advice, feedback, answers to questions, and suggestions for change. However, the mentor does not serve in the manager's role of performance evaluator and—typically—a mentor does not participate in the mentee's performance evaluation—even for casual input. Obviously, if organizations have institutionalized the mentoring process to such an extent that there are one or more questions on the mentee's evaluation form, mentors can participate in the process.
- A mentor cannot guarantee the success of the mentee in their primary position nor within the organization. However, a successful mentorship process is designed to contribute to the success of a mentee in their primary position as well as within the organization in general.
- A mentor cannot provide—no matter the mentee's issues or performance—complete support for all primary work-related activities of mentees. But it is not uncommon for the mentorship process to include—articulated by the mentor/mentee

job descriptions or process outline—specific areas of mentorship needed such as "the mentor guides the mentee through their orientation to the organization as a whole" or "the mentee seeks targeted assistance in a specific area of their position such as budgeting, working remotely with others or with project management."

- A mentor should not operate as a third party and be an alternative way to communicate with a mentee's supervisor. However, a mentorship relationship can include discussion on, orientation to, and training on the employee and manager relationship in organizations, institutions, and associations.

## MENTOR JOB DESCRIPTION WITH ROLES AND RESPONSIBILITIES

Mentor job descriptions should present an overall definition of the mentorship program as well as a mentor's specific roles and responsibilities and *possible* roles and responsibilities. (See examples of job descriptions in appendix B.) Descriptions should be more detailed than an organizational job description and can include choices of activities, percentages of time spent on activities, as well as prioritizations, rankings, or sorting of activities into categories such as primary and secondary. Modes and methods of mentorship activities such as types of upward, downward, and peer or relationship communication, frequency of communication, discussion or interactions, as well as specifics on feedback, progress, and time lines for completing activities should be included.

Mentor styles or types and profiles or examples include unique aspects such as gender, age, culture, and so on. These elements can be identified on applications and can be used to add to the matching process of mentor and mentee.

Mentorship programs and processes should take any unique aspects into account in the identification of mentors and mentees because the "match" or "pairing" of individuals and their unique aspects can enrich a program or relationship. Aspects factored in may be very individual to the organization. Examples might include:

- matching education (presence or lack of levels or types of education);
- matching experience (presence of or lack of experience—both formal and informal);
- matching gender (not necessarily male to male or female to female, but if an individual has never reported to a male supervisor and requests a male supervisor);
- matching age or age within an organization (older or second career or retiring to just beginning or just beginning to mid-career and not retiring); or
- matching backgrounds (pairing two individuals who both have nonprofit experience, or pairing two individuals who are both from other or similar geographic locations).

Mentors as individuals will have different styles and types of mentoring even in very prescribed programs. In addition, different styles and types as well as programs vary by other organizational factors. Styles and types could include:

- *Management styles.* A mentorship with individuals paired where one has experience in collegial management environments and the other is moving from a more autocratic organization to a more collegial environment.
- *Mentor types.* Although it's simplistic, mentors can be either proactive or reactive. Proactivity is highly desired in a mentor in general, *and* while reactive mentors are less successful given the nature of the responsibility of the expert or guide to reach out, reactive mentors whose roles and responsibilities are more like the resident expert whose advice is sought, when needed, can be effective mentors.
- *Leadership styles.* A mentorship with individual pairs where one has been a leader within the organization even though they don't manage anyone and they are paired with someone who manages people but has never led an initiative.
- *Modes and methods styles.* A mentorship where a high-tech mentor is going to accelerate a lower-tech mentee in an organization where people are connected digitally or remotely. Another situation of this type is in an association

where people are paired to groom others for association leadership year round and not just at conferences, or a school district where a more seasoned high school librarian mentors the new high school librarian across town remotely throughout his first year.

Finally, in looking at both titles and definitions, mentorship programs are not just limited to relationships paired within the same sizes and types of libraries. Individuals in solo situations can mentor those in larger situations: public librarians can mentor academic librarians, and school librarians can mentor special librarians. The success of any pairing lies in the identification of relationship goals and the match or pairing of individuals within those goals. The size and type of institution, organization, or association is often not an issue at all or is used to provide the breadth of experiences needed for expanding awareness and understanding.

## WHAT A MENTEE IS OR DOES

Mentees can also be identified by their status such as "first-year circulation staff," "mentee librarian," "junior staff," or "protégé."

Just as in the definition and descriptions of mentors, a program must articulate who and what mentees are and what they do and don't do. Although the majority of definitions of "mentee" define the individual in relationship to the process of mentorship or someone who is "advised, trained, or counseled by a mentor," a closer look at the individual should be taken. That is, the elements or aspects that make a person "interested in," "in need of," "ready," or eligible for this process should be outlined and can include mentees such as:

- new professionals to an organization (example: a new hire);
- professionals new to another area of an organization (examples: an individual new to a branch or a department or a committee or team);
- individuals new to the profession (examples: recent graduates new to the profession in general or a level within a profession such as a library assistant, clerk, or paraprofessional

who has been at one level within an organization and who has gotten a new or different degree and is now—even within the same organization—new to a required master's level and its accompanying increased responsibilities);

- those new to an entity such as an association or membership group typically related to or unique to a profession (examples: new members to an association or new members to an area, service, or element of the association);

- those new to the task at hand (examples: someone who is a member of a group but who is now the leader of the group);

- individuals desiring of or those whose managers desire them to have a new skill or responsibility that suits a mentor process rather than an education, development, or training opportunity; or

- individuals who have been targeted for future activities (examples: those identified as future managers who need exposure to the organization's management styles from a manager's point of view; those being readied for assuming specific management roles).

## WHAT A MENTEE ISN'T AND WHAT A MENTEE DOESN'T DO

Also, just as for mentors, what mentees "aren't" should be identified. Examples include:

- As with mentors—the mentor/mentee relationship could begin as friendship or end up as a friendship but for the mentee, the specific mentorship process isn't a friendship. The attributes that contribute to a successful friendship, however, can be used for mentees, including using mentors for listening and seeking responses, seeking support for mentee projects and activities, and seeking opinions and critiques.

- A mentee should not *expect* a mentor to serve as a "guaranteed" path to promotion or a new position either within or external to the organization. Great care should be taken for mentees to understand what elements of support are available; that is, if mentees can request a reference, that opportunity should be articulated as well as the specific aspects of the reference. If the mentee seeks support for a job that does not relate to the mentorship, the mentee and mentor should be aware of what a mentor could address and not address in supporting activities.

- The mentee should be aware of opportunities for feedback or guidance on performance issues and be aware of opportunities for answers to questions and suggestions for change. However, the mentee must understand that the mentor does *not* serve in the manager's role of performance evaluator and that—typically—a mentor does not participate in the mentee's performance evaluation—even with casual input.

- A mentee cannot expect the mentorship to provide success in his or her primary position in the organization. However, a successful mentorship process is designed to contribute to the success of a mentee within the relationship structure and, possibly, in their primary position within the organization.

- A mentee cannot expect—no matter what their issues or performance—complete support for all of their mentee activities from a mentor. Mentees can and should work with mentors to identify specific areas for program interactions. In addition, it is common for the organization or the mentorship process to provide—by virtue of the mentor/mentee job descriptions or process outline—specific areas of mentee need, such as the mentee being guided through their orientation to the organization as a whole or the mentee receiving targeted assistance within a specific area of their relationship goals such as budgeting, working remotely with others, or project management.

- A mentee should not expect or seek a mentor to operate as a third party and function as, for example, an alternative way to communicate with the mentee's supervisor of their primary job. However, a mentee might have opportunities for (and should seek clarification on the availability of) discussion on, orientation to, and training on the employee and manager relationship in organizations, institutions, and associations.

## MENTEE JOB DESCRIPTION WITH ROLES AND RESPONSIBILITIES

Mentee job descriptions should present an overall definition of the mentorship program as well as a mentee's specific roles and responsibilities and *possible* roles and responsibilities. (See examples of job descriptions in appendix B.) Descriptions should be more detailed than an organizational job description and different from the mentee's job description for their primary job and can include choices of activities, percentage of time spent on activities as well as prioritizations, and rankings or sorting of activities into categories such as primary and secondary. Modes and methods describing mentee activities such as upward, downward, and peer or relationship communication, frequency of communication, discussion or interactions, as well as specifics on feedback, progress, and time lines for completing activities should be included.

Mentee styles and profiles include unique aspects such as gender, age, culture, and so on.

Mentorship programs and processes should take any unique mentee needs or aspects into account in the identification of mentors and in the "match" or "pairing" of individuals. Aspects factored in may be very individual to the organization. Examples might include:

- *Matching education.* A mentee might seek someone with a completely different education to expand their awareness or the same education to allow for increased awareness of how education can be applied to an organization.
- *Matching experience.* A mentee typically seeks someone with greater experience and typically more formal experience, although mentees should be made aware of the benefits of mentors who have both formal and informal experience.
- *Matching unique aspects such as gender, age, backgrounds.* Mentees might seek a path that is different from their own experience or might recognize the value of having alternate mentorship styles and experiences as well as unique perspectives based on life experiences as well as organizational experiences.

Mentees might profit from or have the need of pairings with different styles of mentors and mentoring. In addition, different styles and programs vary by other organizational factors.

Finally—in looking at both titles and definitions—mentorship programs are not just limited to relationships paired within sizes and types of libraries. Programs *must* build in the value factor—program content should include the articulation of benefits and values beyond sizes and types of libraries and librarians. Just as in discussions of success for mentors, successful pairing lies in the identification of relationships and the identification of mentee goals as well as the match or pairing of mentees to mentors who can assist them in meeting those goals.

**REFERENCES**

1. The Coaching and Mentoring Network, www.coachingnetwork.org.uk/information-portal/Articles/ViewArticle.asp?artId=54.
2. Ibid.
3. Ibid.
4. Ibid.
5. ALA Connect, http://connect.ala.org/mentorconnect-help.
6. The Coaching and Mentoring Network.
7. Ibid.
8. Ibid.
9. Ibid.
10. Ibid.
11. Ibid.
12. Ibid.
13. ALA Connect.
14. WebJunction, www.webjunction.org.
15. Minnesota Library Association, Institute for Leadership Excellence, https://sites.google.com/site/mlaexcellence/mentors.

# 2

# THE BREADTH OF TWENTY-FIRST-CENTURY MENTORING

**T**O USE HYPERBOLE and say *everyone* is doing mentoring is almost correct. The professional literature is full of accounts of the "role and value of" of mentoring in not only different types and sizes of environments but in a breadth of professions. And as organizational documentation becomes more prevalent on the Web— many are sharing not only stories and experiences but also extensive explanatory and supporting documentation. And while some elements and activities in mentorship programs do not "move over" or translate for libraries, certain aspects of environments do matter and can have a positive influence on a library mentorship program or process.

## • A CASE METHOD •

### STEPPING UP

Bernice was excited to win her election as vice-chair/chair-elect to the board of her association; however, one of her primary responsibilities was to work with Edward, the board chair, in the appointment of committee chairs and team leaders. Bernice knew that members had been notoriously reticent to step up and accept appointments. In thinking about how she could increase the organization's talent pool, she turned to her own organization's three-year-old mentorship program for new employees and wondered if some of those practices could translate into "building" a sound base of potential committee and team leaders as well as future elected section and board members. But the organizations were disparate, and she was unsure of where to start. In addition, she knew it wasn't her decision only, so not only did she have to outline how it might work, but she had to present and sell the program to the board and especially Edward, the current chair.

## Case Steps/Exploration

1. Read the case thoroughly without underlining or noting case elements. Take no immediate position or role. Then, during the second reading, note elements of the case by underlining or circling case individuals or "characters," case facts as stated, case suppositions, and implied as well as clearly stated issues and actual, perceived, or possible problems.

## STEPPING UP

Bernice was excited to win her election as vice-chair/chair-elect to the board of her association; however, one of her primary responsibilities was to work with Edward, the board chair, in the appointment of committee chairs and team leaders. Bernice knew that members had been notoriously reticent to step up and accept appointments. In thinking about how she could increase the organization's talent pool, she turned to her own organization's three-year-old mentorship program for new employees and wondered if some of those practices could translate into "building" a sound base of potential committee and team leaders as well as future elected section and board members. But the organizations were disparate, and she was unsure of where to start. In addition, she knew it wasn't her decision only, so not only did she have to outline how it might work, but she had to present and sell the program to the board and especially Edward, the current chair.

2. Prepare lists of the important or relevant facts and statements in the situation.
   - Association members need to accept appointments and step up and take leadership roles.
   - Board members are responsible for appointing people to "step up."
   - There are specific issues or problems within the association concerning members "stepping up."
   - There is a longstanding (three-year) program in an organization that a board member is familiar with and willing to explore.
   - Some elements of the organization's program might translate to the association.
   - It's not clear if a board member is unsure of where to start to determine how the program might translate.
   - The idea needs to be presented to board members as they decide together on new programs for the association.

3. List the characters or "players" in the situation, and—if possible—list them in relevant categories such as those directly involved, those indirectly involved, and those affected by the situation. Other categories or descriptors for characters can be: decision makers, primary vs. secondary characters in the case, and so on.
   - Primary categories of players
     Members to be appointed to association roles
     Board member—Bernice
     Board chair—Edward
     Other board members to be in the decision-making process
     The executive director
     Other association leadership
   - Secondary categories of players
     Program designers of the three-year program

Current mentors of the three-year program
Current mentees of the three-year program
Past mentors of the three-year program
Past mentees of the three-year program

4. Review the underlined, marked case elements and list the primary or most important issues, elements, and problems in the case or situation.

## Primary

- There are specific issues or problems within the association concerning members "stepping up."
- Association members need to accept appointments and step up and take leadership roles.
- Some elements of the organization's mentorship program might translate to the association.

## Secondary

- Board members are responsible for appointing people to "step up."
- There is a "longstanding" (three-year) program in an organization that a board member is familiar with/to explore.
- It's not clear/a Board member is unsure of where to start to determine how the program might translate.
- The idea needs to be presented to board members as they decide together on new programs for the association.

5. Prioritize the most important and least important issues or problems in the situation. At this point in case review, the time lines indicated by the case should be taken into consideration. However, other aspects of the case may contribute significantly toward prioritizing case elements. Other ways to prioritize could include: assignment of letters or numbers to indicate hierarchy, now vs. later, immediate vs. can wait, and so on.

There are specific issues/problems within the association concerning members stepping "up."

Association members need to accept appointments and step up and take leadership roles.

Association members need to be interviewed as to why they won't step up to lead.

There is a "longstanding" (three-year) program in an organization that a board member is familiar with/to explore.

It's not clear/a board member is unsure of where to start to determine how the program might translate.

6. After review and discussion of the prioritized situation content, and given the players, elements of the organization, and so on, list "what can be done."

- The board can begin to discuss the problems and issues before the project is presented or completed and should assess (brainstorm? interview?) why members are reticent to step up.
- The board can appoint a small group to explore association issues.
- Bernice's organizational program can and should be assessed and individuals interviewed within both organizations.
- The smaller board group should explore other mentorship programs—reviewing for quality rather than just for a match to their type or size of organization.
- The smaller board group should identify the best elements of the program to apply to the association.
- The smaller board group should work with the executive director (for budget issues, and so on) to explore how the program (more than likely a pilot) can be integrated into the association to set a foundation for the future but yield short-term results as well.

7. After review and discussion of the prioritized situation content, and given the players, elements of the organization, and so on, list "what can't be done."

- Board members can't continue to attempt to appoint without assessing appointment issues and addressing member reticence within the association.

- The organization's program can't be adopted "as is" given the nature of the two different entities.

8. Choose the best one or two solutions given what data is available, and what is missing.
   - The board should immediately discuss the problems and issues as to why members are reticent to step up as well as query board members and others to see what their knowledge base is regarding the specific issue and solutions.
   - The board should appoint a small group to explore association issues as well as other associations and their solutions to the same or similar problems. This group can also look at Bernice's organization since it appears to be successful and she has more in-depth awareness.
   - The smaller board group should include the executive director and should identify the best elements of the program to apply to the association, ensuring that both short-term and longer-term outcomes are planned with significant evaluation.

9. Speculate on the outcome(s) and impact if the solutions are used and put into effect.

## Solution

The board should immediately discuss the problems and issues as to why members are reticent to step up, as well as query board members and others to see what their knowledge base is regarding the specific issue and solutions.

## Outcome Speculations and Impact

Board discussion produces a thoughtful list of issues and ideas as well as collective knowledge on mentorship programs as a possible solution to the lack of leadership and membership reticence.

## Solution

The board should appoint a small group to explore association issues as well as other associations and their solutions to the same or similar problems. This group can also look at Bernice's organization since it appears to be successful and she has more in-depth awareness.

## Outcome Speculations and Impact

The smaller board team (including the executive director) identifies a short-term plan for immediate appointments as well as a foundation for future leadership building and brings the plan to the larger board for approval.

## Solution

The smaller board group should include the executive director and should identify the best elements of the program to apply to the association, ensuring that both short-term and longer-term outcomes are planned with significant evaluation.

## Outcome Speculations and Impact

The program is outlined with significant evaluation during the first year to provide a foundation for a longer-term building block of leaders among members. Build in an evaluation mechanism.

10. Evaluation throughout the program/pilot is critical and should include:
    - identification of association best practices for integrating leadership commitment;
    - evaluation of needs and elements to assess other programs;
    - integration of evaluation components *throughout* the proposed plans;
    - specific, measureable outcomes;
    - development of a cohort of individuals to track and evaluate; and
    - involvement of known program mentors and mentees to assess new pilot program elements.

# MENTORING IN OTHER ORGANIZATIONS

Mentorship programs do not belong to any one type of organization nor are they specific to profit or nonprofit organizations. In addition, they are no more or less successful in one type of organization or another. Instead, the concept of individuals chosen and trained to assist or guide others is decades old and can be found in the widest variety of institutions and organizations.

This "world" of mentoring can be found in the professional literature of other professions and disciplines and in a variety of management areas. Identifying successful programs in other non-library entities is easily done and recommended in order to build the perfect program. In addition, seeking specific information on mentors and the mentor process can be found by using and combining diverse search terms.

"Mentoring" and "mentor process" content can be found in the professional literature of library and information science as well as throughout a number of other professions and disciplines and in a variety of management areas. Older content from all professions (some from the 1970s, and much from the 1980s and the 1990s) is valuable and provides solid background for designing and implementing mentor activities. However, newer content (2001 and beyond) should be integrated into contemporary process or program planning to allow for virtual and digital mentor possibilities and a greater focus on nonprofit and not-for-profit program components.

## SEARCH TERMS

- Most online searches using "mentors" yield significant content in both profit and nonprofit organizations and settings.
- "Mentoring" as a search term yields significant resources and often yields more results than "mentor."
- Fewer usable resources are found under "mentor process," while "mentor program" identifies good applicable general content as well as content that highlights best practice programs and processes.

- While "mentee" yields applicable sources, "protégé" yields usable content as well and is heavily used in profit entities as well as other non-library nonprofits.
- Searching files within "leadership" and "leadership programs" for "mentor" identifies quality resources as well as content that includes extensive documentation of programs.
- Using .edu and .org and .net with other search terms assists in identifying appropriate mentor content.
- Using the keyword "internships" gathers information on both paid and unpaid positions, as well as those that tend to be more "first job"-oriented but can be seen as mentorship opportunities. In fact, there are a few mentor-like programs—especially in larger, nonprofit entities such as nonprofits and government agencies—where internship programs are primarily mentorship programs. While this type of a mentorship program might work in some organizations, this content would be less helpful for outcomes, incentives, and so on as it is uncommon for libraries to be able to promise or even intimate that first-year internships could become a first paid professional position.
- Terms to use besides the obvious "mentor" and "mentorship" that might provide content on mentorship programs are "leadership," "succession planning," "onboarding," "new employees," and "new professionals" as well as "career development."

# ORGANIZATIONS THAT HAVE SIGNIFICANT MENTORSHIP PROGRAMS

### HEALTH SCIENCES ENVIRONMENTS (HOSPITALS, EDUCATION PROGRAMS SUCH AS NURSING SCHOOLS, AND SO ON)

A wide variety of medical and health settings have integrated mentor programs into not only education and training but orienting new employees and moving employees around in organizations. Mentorship programs work especially well in health care environments, where evidence-based curriculum is supplemented with one-on-one and small group discussion and role modeling among cohorts and peers. Mentorship programs are especially successful in these programs where an integral part of study is rotation among departments or subject areas for intense observation of experts or organizational "seniors." Libraries can learn from these programs overall but especially in their rotation processes and in their outcomes-based curriculum. In addition, these programs have extensive supplementary mentee learning through peer discussions among mentees with a focus on active learning.

## ASSOCIATIONS

The business of associations cannot be carried out without membership, specifically *active* membership and membership assistance. The successful association is one that identifies need and talents to integrate the growing of association leaders into the business of the organization. Mentorship programs in associations develop individuals throughout the organization as well as association officers and support for conference or meeting assistance. While many members are "mentored" to learn how to support conference or event activities, the bulk of association mentorship is for building organizational leaders.

Library associations are active and avid users of mentoring to build middle-level and higher-level leaders. In addition, library organizations in states and regions institute mentoring programs to build an active membership and expand their members' leadership potential. Many regional library organizations offer intense and often weeklong immersions for initial short-term membership training that grow into substantive professional networks.

## HIGHER EDUCATION

Educators have been guiding others within institutions for many years. The classic higher education mentor relationship has been between the tenured faculty member and the non-tenured faculty member, and many programs have been implemented to assist women and diverse faculty. These mentor/mentee relationships have provided success for leading others in the research and publication process, grantsmanship, teaching and learning, and in service to the institution and the community. Higher education has also hosted extensive, in-depth mentoring in applying other roles and responsibilities—such as development—and on teaching and learning activities for new pedagogies such as distance learning and pedagogies appropriate for special populations. Academic libraries also provide extensive mentorship programs and opportunities both in tenure and non-tenure situations for—as classroom faculty—the research and publication process, grantsmanship, teaching and learning, and in service to the institution and the community. In addition, academic libraries provide extensive mentorship program content online.

## CORPORATE SETTINGS

Although corporate environments are often competitive environments for employees, mentorship programs are often used to expand employee experiences across departments as well as provide management and leadership experiences for individuals with management education but no experience. Corporate America has implemented mentoring (identified as mentoring as well as coaching and internships) in organizations of all sizes. The benefits of corporate mentorship programs include providing employees opportunities for fast-tracking careers, general career development, improving leadership skills, improving management skills, assisting diverse employees in career development, and providing opportunities for technical or unique knowledge and employee retention. Libraries can learn from corporate mentorship programs' focus on diversity and unique employee populations.

## BUREAUCRACIES

Bureaucracies are typically defined as organizations that carry out the business of government (local, state, regional, or federal) and are characterized by a variety of levels of hierarchy. A growing number of mentorship programs in these organizations provide opportunities for promising employees to move among the variety of departments and functions with the goal of future employment at higher and the highest levels of management and leadership positions. Additional opportunities exist through mentor opportunities for those with content expertise (government policy, social service practice, and agency business such as environment) and functional expertise (budgeting, planning) who need process expertise such as management or communication. Libraries can learn from bureaucratic organizations' mentorship program practices of rotating mentees among departments for both organizational as well as functional learning opportunities.

## COMMON GOALS OF MENTORSHIP PROGRAMS

The *focus* of some of the most successful mentorship programs today—no matter what the organization or entity—include the following.

### DIVERSITY

Many mentorship programs strive to recruit and mentor individuals who are from underrepresented groups in order to enhance diversity within organizations. Mentoring expands opportunities for individuals to increase competencies, and to build leaders of color, ethnicity, race, and culture as well as leaders from different backgrounds, different geographical regions, and representing different age levels and gender differences.

### LEADERSHIP

Leadership is one of the primary areas of focus of mentorship programs no matter what the type or size of the institution or entity. Although leadership content varies dramatically across organizations, using a mentor/mentee process to illustrate and educate potential leaders can be replicated in almost all organizations. The content of leadership is especially well-suited to the mentor process because some of the most successful leadership curricula are delivered through observation and role modeling.

## GENDER ISSUES

Gender issues—now categorized more as diversity issues—reflect a variety of hiring, promotion, and retention issues in organizations where it appears that gender determines whether or not an individual is eligible for hire or for promotion. In addition, organizations lose talent when those individuals—frustrated by lack of progress—seek employment elsewhere.

## LEGAL PROFESSION

Although the legal profession is often characterized as an excessively competitive one, mentorship programs abound for new attorneys as well as in larger organizations. These mentorships focus on providing opportunities for new attorneys to seek feedback on challenging work as well as providing support on balancing personal and work life as well as productivity.

## FAMILY AND YOUTH WITH CHALLENGES

Extensive mentorship opportunities exist throughout the workforce in organizations that provide support for families and youth in challenging environments and situations. Many of these programs have—given the nature of the client—in-depth learning and training that focus on extensive curriculum on the family and society, the developmental needs of the client by age, lifestyle, education; background, and so on; as well as learning and training for those working with the client and the client's family. The programs are also characterized by more frequent mentor and mentee face-to-face activities—especially in the preliminary stages, as well as both meetings and *more* meetings in general with those adjacent to the client such as caregivers, parents, and so on. Mentorship programs for these client groups include more extensive requirements and preparation, including reference checks and criminal background checks.

## PROFESSIONALS IN TARGET POPULATIONS

An interesting aspect to mentorship programs designed for individuals desiring learning and expanded opportunities is the focus on mentees interested in working with other employees and workers in unique categories including those sorted by age, experience, and education as well as preferences for work environments and work styles. In addition, these programs offer mentorship opportunities to individuals who desire to be mentors and who represent these same categories to expand the organization or institution's "population" of employees.

## ISOLATION/SOLITARY POPULATIONS

Mentorship programs are especially successful when providing alternative work opportunities for those in limited situations. And while the obvious description of the environment is someone who works alone in the organization, these programs are also for those who might be the only one in the organization doing a specific job or the only one with a certain responsibility or level of education or training.

## EMERGING CAREERS AND CONTENT

A growing number of mentorship programs include connections among people who work in new, emerging, and changing careers. Examples include areas where there might be very little formal education as well as where there is—very likely—only one person in the organization familiar with the content. Examples include sustainability or green careers as well as areas like STEM or STEAM.

## DIGITAL AND VIRTUAL MODES AND METHODS

Although one might imagine that rural or more geographically isolated areas are the focus of primary digital or virtual as well as hybrid mentorship programs, in contemporary society a digital/virtual or hybrid mentorship program can be in place when mentors or mentees are—literally—in the same building. These modes and methods provide opportunities for more frequent interactions, online curriculum content for study, and teaching and learning spaces including course management software as well as wikis and blogs. Obviously, the digital/virtual world offers easier, more frequent communication as well as the creation of online work spaces and expanded documentation.

## MENTORING IN ASSOCIATIONS, CLUBS, AND MEMBERSHIP GROUPS

Obviously a frequent use of mentorship in the library profession—exclusive of institutions—is in associations. In fact, mentor processes have been a constant in associations for many years, and while mentoring in institutions doesn't exactly mirror association mentoring, the basic definitions apply and include individuals who take special or personal interests in less experienced individuals; those who impart knowledge, skills and abilities, and attitudes; and those with a strong desire to see others grow, develop, and succeed. Mentor activities in associations have diverse modes and methods of delivery and include curricula designed for education and training, self-reflection, journaling, and the use of various pedagogies to meet the needs of not only the association but the individual. Even with the similarities of definitions to mentoring in institutions, however, mentor processes cannot be characterized by any one specific approach or program, such as informal vs. formal, short-term or long-term, or year-round or conference-only processes. Rather, association mentoring is better explained through a listing of possible activities and then descriptions of types of programs existing in associations today.

With any descriptions of mentoring programs, the expectation might be that an organization could vet program examples and then choose from among the examples for the best match to their own environment. The reality is, however, that a very wide variety of program elements are present and organizations must pick and choose from among elements to build their own mentoring programs given the size of their membership; membership longevity; the presence or dearth of future leaders (officers, project coordinators, committee or work group leaders such as task force leaders), organizational budgets; the size of association "territory" such as state, multistate, or region; the "type" of member (type of library, functional areas of the profession, and so on); organizational technological infrastructure and expertise; facilities; staff size; staff expertise; organizational goals; constituent needs; or geographic issues.

Just as in institutional mentoring, association mentoring can be *informal* with relationships between or among association members formed in the absence of an articulated process or at lower association levels; *formal* with a process in place and supported by the association; short term (either formal or informal) with a *process in place* but relationships either shorter and designed for projects, or activities or longer relationships to support the acquisition of knowledge; facilitated for typically more than one mentor and more than one mentee; *group mentoring* in which departments, groups, or multiple mentors are involved; c*o-mentoring* using two mentors for an individual in an activity; or *virtual, digital, or e-mentoring* for exclusively online practices or for a mix or hybrid of modes and methods for delivery.

Association mentoring processes, activities, and elements include but are not limited to activities that increase membership success and commitment by enhancing membership experiences at conferences in general, experiences at conferences for specific interests, experiences that support specific career development such as conference or continuing education content for promotion, tenure, moving up in management and finding that next perfect position, as well as general networking for both professional relationships and professional friendships. In addition, mentoring takes place at all levels within associations, including new member mentoring for overall association success and sustaining members; middle-level leadership mentor-to-mentee processes for chairs and team leaders for committees, task forces, other work groups, and project management; high-level leadership mentor-to-mentee processes for officer-level experiences; and infrastructure mentors working with mentees (technology, communication, conference business, association business, strategic planning, project management, and so on). These experiences can include but are not limited to a variety of arrangements such as:

- one-to-one mentor-to-mentee relationships;
- one to small group mentor-to-mentees opportunities;
- peer mentoring with paired individuals with matched interest or goals;
- group mentoring (with one or more mentors and several or more mentees); and
- team mentoring (for knowledge-based groups identified to work with individuals for "minute," short-term, project, or longer-term mentoring).

And any of these activities can use a variety of modes and methods and include:

- all in-person mentor-to-mentee activities;
- all digital/virtual mentor-to-mentee activities; and
- hybrid/mix of in-person and digital/virtual mentor-to-mentee activities.

# THE VALUE AND BENEFITS OF MENTORING

**T**HERE ARE MANY aspects of management and leadership we can't cost out; however, designing and implementing support mechanisms for our employees, workers, and members is something we shouldn't avoid—no matter what the cost. In fact, the argument might be made that we shouldn't even try to identify costs—and while many would agree that it is counterproductive to spend extensive time identifying dollars spent, the *value and benefits* of mentoring *should* be identified.

The mentor question we all *don't* ask but should is: What specific value does mentoring bring to the table?

Although beginning a first mentor pilot program won't cost significant, actual dollars in budgets (in most cases,) it *will* cost valuable staff time and a commitment of people.

Given scarce staff development and continuing education dollars, mentor programs *do* provide in-depth educational opportunities for individuals but costs must include—as in other areas—staff time and in many cases extensive staff time.

Since we often don't know what the benefits or value of mentoring are before we begin or what our "return" might be, should we begin the program? *Yes,* and to determine "return," outcomes that include individual achievement, performance, and products should be used to identify program directions and thus, program success.

Designing and implementing any new program in libraries of any type and size involves money. Programs that seemingly "don't cost the organization any money" *do* cost money in organization time from the initial phase throughout the implementation, maintenance, and evaluation process. While it is often hard—without specific dollar amounts—to predict the return on value of activities, the design phase should include a needs assessment that outlines current or potential or actual upcoming problems within the organization and how possible programs or relationships will either solve or contribute to the solution of problem through the establishment of outcomes.

As with any program—if organizational issues include the budget—with either real or "time spent" dollars, organizations should start small with a pilot mentoring program. Smaller programs should focus on one set of goals. Examples of these include orientation for all new employees or onboarding new librarians, expanding awareness of management opportunities within the organization, and a limited number of both mentors and mentees. Additional elements for a soft or slower start include very narrowly defined and measureable outcomes or "returns" as well as more project-oriented, shorter-term opportunities with tight time lines.

Measureable benefits, outcomes, and returns should be articulated with appropriate terminology and appropriate measurement of change with evaluative techniques such as broad ranges of numerical-only Likert scales as well as annotated Likert scales.

## ORGANIZATIONAL BENEFITS AND VALUE OF TWENTY-FIRST-CENTURY MENTORSHIP

Although the concept of the mentor and the mentee has been around for hundreds of years and we know much about the world of "mentoring" or "mentorship," there are still *many* mysteries about the process. This area of human resources or organizational development, management, or leadership is not unlike the story of the blind men and the elephant in the middle of the room . . . everyone sees or feels differently about the issue. And much of what we think about the issue is based on personal experiences or organizational experiences we have had or observed.

No matter what the environment, however, mentorship benefits and values are significant. Twenty-first-century mentorship outcomes, "return," and values and benefits for organizations and institutions in general include:

- *Expanded competencies.* Mentoring passes expertise to those who need to acquire specified skills to assist with or go beyond the competencies required for the primary position's roles and responsibilities.
- *Education to practice.* Mentoring addresses the gap between theory and practice for recent graduates with little or no time spent in practice.
- *Professionalism.* Mentoring provides constructs for the tenets of professionalism and what it means to be a professional in their profession and includes the importance of ethics and ethical behavior, and the need for trust between and among mentorship participants.
- *Orientation, onboarding, acculturation process.* Mentoring assists those new to the organization or position to become acclimated to the organization or institution.
- *Career development.* Mentoring provides support for career management and planning.
- *Organizational development.* Mentoring communicates the vision, mission, values, and goals of the organization.
- *Retention.* Mentoring provides the necessary information and experience to allow professionals to fully experience the profession to facilitate recruitment and retention.
- *Knowledge transfer.* Mentoring provides opportunities for the interchange and exchange of knowledge between and among senior and junior members of the organization.

And specifically:

- expertise shared across organizations and departments;
- supplementation of training, education, and development in economically challenged environments;
- experience in specialty areas that are taught less frequently

in many formal programs (examples: seniors, young adults, special needs constituents, and so on);

- support for solo librarian environments;
- training, education, and support for librarians in libraries without educational credentials such as graduate credentials if appropriate, required, or desired by the institution;
- different practice or practical support for education programs with online-only or distance learning students;
- time-saving for orientation and training in organizations with new employees, high turnover, or significant numbers of volunteers, as well as for associations when mentors serve to support intermittent or less frequent events and activities;
- education to provide opportunities to "ready" upwardly mobile employees in organizations;
- assistance with general career transition across types and sizes of libraries;
- assistance in understanding requirements for job success such as research and publication in general as well as tenure requirements, successful performance evaluation, and pathways to promotion;
- awareness of organizational politics, the bureaucratic processes of the organization, sociometrics, organizational lore, and organizational tradition;
- opportunities for discussions without involving direct managers or management for discussions on expectations, to bring up sensitive issues, vent, gather perspectives from diverse areas of the organization, or for touchstones to identify standard practices and deviations from standard practice;
- networking for contacts for current work and lifelong professional networking, for advice on career development including professional involvement and specifics such as online presence, general résumé information, and references for work, research, service, and so on;
- expanded self-confidence for all involved in the program;
- assistance in learning about and navigating content areas needed but not covered in previous education or experience;

- awareness or increased awareness of the profession (library and information science, profit vs. nonprofit) for employees educated or trained in other professions;
- increased number of individuals ready to step up to take positions within the organization or association with evidence of increased applicants, increased successful applicants, more candidates taking leadership positions with associations, and more candidates available to stand for or run for office;
- expanded content opportunities for practice and field experience programs across all types and sizes of libraries;
- expanded numbers of digital and virtual mentorship opportunities exist for expanding programs beyond metropolitan areas and larger institutions and organizations;
- expanded numbers of short-term mentorship activities such as tech training, project management, management, or leadership to expand expertise either as an enhancement or substitute for continuing education or development opportunities;
- expanded opportunities for designing teaching and learning opportunities for special, unique, or smaller populations;
- expanded opportunities for varying levels of employees in organizations including support staff, non-library staff, employees without advanced degrees, senior employees, and diverse employees;
- increased recruitment, retention, and sustainability of association membership;
- greater network of individuals committed to management and leadership training in general and a greater network of those who want to manage and lead in associations and organizations;
- increased leadership training and education with associations to create member leaders for increased service;
- expanded access to expertise and opportunities for enhanced virtual or digital mentor processes; and
- greater success and numbers in retention of library employees and workers.

# THE BENEFITS FOR THE MENTOR

Although many would tell you that mentees get the greatest benefit from the mentorship program, mentors will tell you that they receive just as many if not more benefits from the experience, such as:

- exposure to new or expanding ideas and interests;
- professional challenges;
- satisfaction in sharing a competency set such as professional knowledge, tech skills and abilities, and attitudes such as commitment and enthusiasm;
- identification and expanding of effective and best practices that cause individuals to reflect on existing practices;
- feedback and critical analysis resulting in growth and development;
- opportunity to practice developmental behaviors outside one's own direct line responsibilities;
- development of one's own self-awareness;
- heightened awareness of challenges and issues at different levels within the organization;
- greater understanding of other library organizations and library roles; and
- learning from the shared interactions with mentors and mentees.

# THE BENEFITS FOR THE MENTEE

The benefits of mentoring for the mentee include many of the same if not similar benefits for mentors, such as

- exposure to new or expanding ideas and interests;
- professional challenges;
- satisfaction in learning a competency set such as professional knowledge, tech skills and abilities, and attitudes such as commitment and enthusiasm;

- identification and expanding of effective and best practices that cause individuals to understand the value of best practices early in their career;
- feedback and critical analysis resulting in growth and development unique to mentee needs;
- opportunity to practice developmental behaviors outside one's own direct line of responsibilities;
- development of one's own self-awareness;
- heightened awareness of challenges and issues at different levels within the organization;
- greater understanding of other library organizations and library roles; and
- learning from the shared interactions with mentors and mentees.

In addition, mentees become more motivated to succeed in their job as well as in the organization and in the profession. They become more self-aware of their own needs and also of their own talents and how they can contribute to the organization and the profession. They acquire a more in-depth knowledge of the profession. Besides these benefits, mentoring gives mentees a process for and a commitment to continuing education and professional development; experience in learning cohorts; introduction to applications of the tenets of the profession such as ethical behavior; and expanded training in communication and leadership.

## EVEN NON-PARTICIPANTS BENEFIT

An additional set of outcomes that should be articulated but seldom are include those that benefit and provide value to individuals *not* involved in the mentorship program. While these are often ignored, they are a critical part of acceptance of the program. For those *not* involved, benefits and values for institutions can include:

- heightened awareness of the importance of orientation and initial training of employees;

- role modeling of critical relationships needed to attract and sustain diverse employees;
- reduced training and continuing education time for many employees who—previous to the mentorship program—were responsible for working with individuals outside their area of expertise;
- the existence of an increased knowledge-base for employees; and
- increased expertise in critical roles in the organization affecting all others, such as more expert, technologically responsible employees or improved performance with infrastructure technology.

Association members not involved in mentorship programs have more easily identified benefits and values including:

- members ready and able for conference involvement;
- members ready and able for general service involvement such as committee, division, council, round table, and so on, active membership, leadership, and project management;
- members ready and able to run or stand for office and appointment; and
- members ready to share their professional expertise with others through presentation and publication as well as design of curriculum for other association members.

Finally and obviously, observing the value and benefits or overall success of mentorship in any environment and at any level assists in "growing" both future mentors and mentees in the widest variety of experiences possible.

# DESIGNING AND IMPLEMENTING MENTORSHIP PROGRAMS AND PROCESSES

**A**LTHOUGH IT STANDS to reason that the smaller the program or the fewer the number of mentors and mentees, the less structure or paperwork you need, the reality is that—no matter the size of the initiative—structure and documentation are needed to institutionalize the activities. Beyond just "effective management practice," other issues driving the design of effective structure and content include for institutions:

- Activities—although typically *not* part of someone's primary work for the organization—*are* done on work time and as such must be articulated appropriately.
- The presence of structure contributes to the overall success of mentorship because it provides support for not only goals or outcomes but also issues and challenges as they arise.

In associations, structure and documentation is critical due to the typically disparate nature of association activities, the frequent lack of staff in associations, and the reliance on membership for carrying out initiatives. In addition, the increasing use of online or hybrid activities needs structure to provide organization for communication among the individuals involved. Finally, structure and documentation offer much-needed accountability for mentorship activities to assist in the measurement of the success of goals and outcomes.

## THE MENTOR QUESTION #1

We have two smaller and two larger branch libraries in rural, more isolated areas but we really need to provide support for these two managers—one new and one seasoned but from another area. Should I provide a mentorship program with these managers and—if yes—how?

Contemporary mentorship programs are greatly enhanced by the use of digital/virtual mentoring opportunities. And while the jury is still out on the "long look" at all-online mentorship activities, there are great opportunities for success in carefully planned all-online, hybrid activities as well as electronic communication used for in-person mentorship programs. The primary question here, however, is "What are the goals of the program?" That is, the question states that the organization wants to "provide support" for the managers. Management needs to decide if the "support" is for the managers' primary job roles and responsibilities or their development within the organization. If support is more for development, the program might contain best practices (rather than organization expectations) to communicate with supervisors remotely; building teams in isolation; or staying part of the larger team of the library in remote environments. Additional mentorship content should also include paths for the two managers to network with each other to share successes and challenges as well as what best practices work for them.

The "how" part of the question might be answered with:

- Does the library have a larger mentorship program to piggyback on? And can it be converted to a digital/virtual program for employees in remote locations?
- Are best practices available from other organization in similar situations?

- Does the library have an online presence where employees can share information? If not, can the staff access free online communication venues from their network? Is it acceptable to create a free online environment for employees that is outside the network?
- Management needs to determine the goals of the activities, then meet with the two managers to identify differences between the primary work roles and responsibilities and mentorship program needs. A mentorship coordinator or process owner needs to be appointed from the organization's overall management team to oversee the design of mentorship processes.

## THE MENTOR QUESTION #2

I want to informally mentor a new assistant manager. I don't need any paperwork, do I?

The easy answer is "it's up to you" if you want to have either an informal or formal program, but the broader, bigger answers should cover the following.

Who are "you?" It is not recommended that supervisors mentor direct reports, so if you are the manager and the new assistant manager reports directly to you, the mentorship process does not work efficiently and actually may interfere with primary job roles and responsibilities for both the manager and the assistant manager. If the organization provides other managers, then one of those should be the mentor. If the organization is not large enough *or* if the other managers are not appropriate for mentorship processes, then a remote mentorship could be considered. In addition, while a manager might work well, given the goals and outcomes desired, another assistant manager, either internal or external to the organization (online, through a consortium, with an association, and so on) might be the answer.

Not all mentor programs have extensive paperwork; however, the more structure the program offers and the more documentation available, the more measurements can be taken and more assessment is possible. Therefore, the mentorship agreement should be in writing (for the mentor and the mentee) as well as general mentorship goals and the communication needed to sustain the relationship.

# DESIGNING FOR POSITIVE RELATIONSHIPS

Designing and implementing in-person, virtual/digital, and hybrid mentorship programs and processes is not an easy task. And—as it is with any program planning—before you outline the plan, you outline goals and outcomes needed. In the case of a mentorship program, this involves characterizing the aspects of a successful mentor and mentee relationship and then primary activities become the "design of" the mentor and the mentee roles and responsibilities as part of the process. While there is some variance by type and size of institution or association, there are a number of characteristics identified throughout the literature on what makes a mentorship relationship successful. Better or best practice relationships in general are characterized by:

- overall planning by the organization as well as an articulated, written plan;
- a time line;
- a communication plan either by itself or within the written plan;
- identification of all employee roles (do and don't do);
- a substantive process for matching of mentors to mentees, including a match or pairing of all those involved, and assessment such as self-identification of preferences and skill sets;
- teaching and learning education and training for mentors and mentees;
- awareness information as well as teaching and learning education and training for the overall organization;
- in-person as well as hybrid infrastructures for groups or more than duos or pairs (examples: forums, panels, blogs, wikis) for content delivery and discussion;

- in-person as well as hybrid infrastructures for duos or pairs of mentors/mentees (examples: in-person and online meetings, blogs, wikis as well as participation in larger events where duos or pairs all come together in a cohort) for content delivery and discussion;
- content integrated within organizational content (vision, mission, goals, outcomes, and plans);
- assessment and evaluation throughout the experience and content; and
- written goals, outcomes, management, mentor and mentee expectation statements for all involved.

## MENTORSHIP PLANNING

Although many mentoring programs seem relatively simple in concept, there are many aspects to planning a two-person mentorship, a smaller activity or initiative, or a pilot, much less a larger mentorship program and processes. To ensure that all aspects of program planning are considered, the following "plan for planning" is offered with recommendations for whatever size program is found to be the best match.

### How Will Planning the Mentorship Program Take Place in the Organization?

In order to adequately plan for mentorship programs, institutions and organizations need to first decide who will coordinate the process of planning. Although implementation may well be coordinated by another group—after initial planning—the first planning group should include a variety of levels of employees throughout the organization in order to illustrate an interest and possible commitment in the process from the beginning of the discussion. This variety of levels of employees should include individuals throughout the organization, including those who are not eligible to be either mentors or mentees. These individuals—tangentially involved or often not involved at all—need to be in on both initial planning as well as implementation in order to have a transparent process that from the beginning focuses on overall benefits and values. While an individual *can* lead the group, a co-chair or co-leader arrangement can assist in not only addressing the variety of people who need to be involved, but also a transition from one planning group to another.

### Once the Mentorship Program Is Planned, Who Will Implement the Initiative?

While the primary planning group *can* be the implementing group, either a broader or sometimes different group can be brought together to not only vet the plan, but carry it out. This second group might be led by one of the co-chairs of the initial group with selected membership.

Obviously "who" is driven by the size and type of the environment. In any situation except when there isn't a critical mass of staff or in smaller institutions and organizations, a planning team of partners and stakeholders can come together either online or in person along with employees to plan or implement or both. Certainly in association environments, planning teams are from diverse environments representing the broadest membership, no matter what the focus of the mentorship program.

Many larger programs in larger institutions and organizations such as large libraries, large school districts, or disparate organization locations as well as associations will want to consider a "process owner" or "coordinator," or at the very least, a designated person who might be chair or team leader of the implementation team, to shepherd the first year of the program. Post first-year, many organizations reduce the amount of time the coordinator focuses on mentoring but retains the position for continuity and post assessment and data gathering.

### What Is the Purpose of the Mentorship Plan?

Mentorship plans are designed to articulate the vision, mission, and goals of the program as well as identify program outcomes. The plan should not only provide an overview for the organization, but for the appropriate, broader audience. It should also have a match of information and activities to budget expenditure and can be broad in content, but specific to processes that need to and will be taking place.

*Who Is the Audience for Content about the Mentorship Program?*
The audience includes all library employees and library workers, umbrella organizations, partners and stakeholders, and—as appropriate—constituents. While it is a given that the primary and secondary planning groups will be using the plan, mentors and mentees will use it as their information and infrastructure as well.

*How Are Time Lines Infused into the Plan?*
Planning time lines need to include timing or the planning itself for both primary planning, and then the implementation group. Other timing issues include:

- Timing for the mentorship program is critical and includes before, during, and after with specific attention paid to measurement and assessment for program evaluation time lines for both the short term, long term, and pilot—if a pilot is considered to be an effective first "year." Additional time lines in the plan are needed for mentor and mentee processes.
- Plan calendars should be dynamic because the mentorship world changes frequently and the specific program morphs pending reviews of program assessment.

*What Is the Best Format or Means of Production?*
Program plans should be primarily online with a design that allows for printing plan sections; for example, for mentor processes and mentee processes. Primarily online content allows for easy updating and ensures there is no (typically inevitable) confusion over "who has what version."

*What Style of Writing Should Be Used for the Mentorship Program Plan?*
Although the institution's or organization's administration should offer a (typically) brief narrative vision and mission statement, the program plan's writing approach should be primarily technical writing with sample documents for personalizing content unique to mentor and mentee relationships.

## How Will You Present the Final Plan?

The final support should be seen as not only a design of the program infrastructure but also as a marketing tool for the audience in regard to the institution's or organization's commitment to mentorship.

## How Will You Distribute?

Distribution should match target audiences so that those audiences using technology should be able to access content online and those audiences not yet online should have copy available in print. A marketing and outreach plan should be located in the final plan and should be designed to drive distribution.

## Content

Does the text both state and reflect the overall purpose of the organization or institution's purpose?

The final plan should begin with the vision, mission, and goals identified. It should also connect or track back to the umbrella institution's overarching vision, mission, goals, and outcomes with similar directions and terminology as well as explain how the mentor program fits into the organization's overall plan for the mentorship program.

## Have You Included an Abstract or Executive Summary?

No plan should be without an abstract, executive summary, or—for example—infographic of the plan's program and process and how it benefits the organization. In fact, there can be several introductory pieces written that have different foci—based on the distribution audience. In addition to brief narrative, this preliminary piece should include unique data that illustrates program outcomes and successes proposed and when realized—articulated.

## Does the Report/Information Tell a Story?

Telling the story of the benefits of the program and process to the organization is tied to the audience—as was the abstract or executive summary. That is, the administration—seeking economical ways to expand professional development—should be told about the "economical" story or direct or indirect cost savings, enhanced professional development, and so on. An audience seeking ways to recruit and retain for upcoming or new hires might be told the story of investment in staff or providing opportunities for growth.

### Are Appendixes Needed?

Appendixes provide space for content that is illustrative or that expands the plan's technically written content. Appendixes should be used for referring those interested in more data to more and unique data. References to appendixes should be within the text of the plan, rather than only providing a laundry list of additional information. Appendixes should have sample documents used in the program as well as any budget information appropriate for public information, a glossary, a list of those involved in the process, research and references, and any evaluative content.

### Cover

The plan's cover should be informative and have excerpted data and—as stated previously—an infographic or meaningful data representation or quote or an unusual or heretofore unknown fact. Although it stands to reason that plans are not necessarily inviting anyway, the cover should provide interesting content to cause the audience to want to learn more.

In addition, there is typically great success in naming or branding and identifying programs and thus the plans. This branding technique unifies the educational cohort of mentors and mentees and also provides slogan opportunities for those involved. Logos also unify the process and are typically derivative of the brand and slogan. Program names—discussed in chapter 1—lend themselves to branding, slogans, and logos.

### Visuals

Visuals used should carry out the theme, be copyright clear, look professional, be labeled appropriately, and explain or complement the text. Plan designers should take great care to gather and present accurate data and to match the outcomes sought and achieved to data-gathering processes and products. Data should be multileveled and not "flat" or one dimensional. As an example, "How many mentees applied to the program" is of less interest than "42 percent of members in the association's 'New Manager's Round Table' applied to be in the Association's first mentorship 'Great First Steps' cohort."

### Distribution

Individuals needing copies of the document include not only those in the program and program planners, but also those in the umbrella organization, partners, stakeholders, and members of the institution or organization's community. In addition, any vendor, funders, or donors and anyone involved in training program members should receive the document. Program administrators and coordinators should identify those who receive it—who needs a presentation of content or at the very least answers to questions.

### Virtual/Digital and Hybrid Mentorship Programs

Although many types of educational programs, continuing education, and professional development are all online today, completely online mentorship programs are more in their early stages, early years, or infancy. It stands to reason, however, that all-online mentoring programs are becoming increasingly easier to manage. There is less or no expense for a growing number of web-based tools that can host webinars or meetings both synchronous and asynchronous; cloud products for content storage; project work spaces such as wikis for sharing curriculum and projects; blogs for journaling; team work space and tracking for projects; media streaming environments to house video and podcast streams for content delivery, teaching, and learning, archived program activities, and advising sessions; and e-mail for general correspondence as well as mentor or mentee or group threaded discussions. Other web-based tools can host web page packages for backdrops for individual or group mentee projects; calendars for posting time lines and processes for individuals or teams; photo-sharing pictures for team building and post-event learning activities or to chronicle conversations, meetings, and so on; course management software to teach a class or cohort of learners with posting, discussion, pushing out notifications, and so on; guides or paths for organizing posted content for reading assignments or for creating forums for projects; and survey environments to assist program planners in assessing and evaluating program elements, participants, and others involved either actively or tangentially.

### But What Is Virtual or Digital or E-Mentoring?

All online programs—typically identified as e-mentoring—are online, software-mediated relationships and activities between or among mentors and mentees designed to provide mentorship opportunities such as advising, teaching and learning, problem solving, training, and overall support for mentorship activities. All-online mentorship programs differ from in-person programs in a number of areas that include some obvious and some not-so-obvious ways, including the following:

- expanded boundaries for all areas are available such as type of library, size of organization, and geographic disparity;
- more specificity in time lines should be articulated to ensure consistent contact;
- matched skilled levels in tech or communication environments are critical to ensure program success;
- more contacts overall can be made if tech competencies are current;
- more guidelines for specific communications are required to adhere to program progression and achieve successful outcomes;
- systematic labeling of program communication (subject headings, and so on);
- a built-in variety of communication (phone, e-mail, some chat, and so on); and
- more protocols for communication.

### What Are the Challenges to Virtual/Digital or E-Mentoring?

Although an "all-online" approach is new and supported by a majority of participants, a variety of evaluative studies as well as anecdotal data are available and identify some problems that include:

- the varieties and types of communication required cannot be mastered by all;

- lower levels of proficiency with the variety and types of communication;
- stricter time lines given the online forums;
- two-way, in-person communication is easier than a two-way tech platform;
- lack of spontaneity driven by reliance on existing technology;
- not everyone is at the same level of technology;
- complaints that the faculty often do not use the myriad of tech tools or do not use them in a timely or correct fashion; and
- desire for at least one or more face-to-face activities.

### What Is a Hybrid Mentorship Program?

One can address what a hybrid mentorship program is by coming at the issue from two perspectives. That is:

- it is an in-person program that is supported by a communication plan that includes a wide variety of online tools, or
- it is an online program that has—for example—"four in-person activities annually" including a preliminary face-to-face, two continuing education events attached to the statewide association's two meetings—and a final evaluative session.

Hybrids exist with online issues being employed primarily to discuss curriculum, training, and peer discussions. While many contemporary mentors might be excluded for their lack of knowledge about the technology being used, technology as a means to an end should be a reality in working with today's employees.

# MENTORSHIP EDUCATION AND TRAINING

**A**S MOST THINGS should, the design of mentorship education and training should begin with people; that is, after organizational need is assessed and articulated, the next step is identifying the education and training needed for all people involved. In this case, "all" is more than a mentor and mentee and includes:

- awareness education for administrators and managers;
- awareness education for appropriate individuals in the umbrella organization;
- awareness education for internal (to the structure of the organization) boards;
- knowledge education and governing (and if entities are governing, impact training as well);
- impact awareness education for employees *not* designated as mentors or mentees or scheduled to orient or train (example: how do the program and individuals impact those *not* in the program?);
- impact awareness education for workers (example: volunteers) *not* designated as mentors or mentees or scheduled to orient or train; and
- skills/abilities training.

# ELEMENTS OF A MENTORSHIP CURRICULUM

Although most organizations and mentors and mentees have differ-ent, customized curriculum needs in organizations, there are core training needs for every mentorship program. These core training needs encompass everything each participant must know—first about the program itself, then about forming and keeping the rela-tionship, then about individual roles and responsibilities, and then finally, based on each individual's needs. The identification, design, and matching of curriculum materials are important steps in the successful preparation of mentees. Curriculum areas can include but are not limited to the following.

## CONTENT

- Content on the profession and professionalism (tenets of being a professional, ethical codes, standards, need for trust, importance of confidentiality)
- Content to establish context for the type and size of library
- Content for the organization hosting the program
- Content for organizations that are active partners in the program
- Content on mentorship as a process
- Content on the mentorship program of the institution (vision, mission, goals, values, outcomes, rules, and regulations)
- Content on the roles and responsibilities of mentors (goals and outcomes)
- Content on the roles and responsibilities of mentees (goals and outcomes)
- Core content on the match and individual profiles of those in the match
- Core content on learning styles and teaching styles in general
- Core content on the learning and teaching styles of the mentors and mentees in the program
- Core content on communication (including modes and methods as well as techniques of communication)

- Core content such as first-year experience as an employee, career development, work patterns, work styles, productivity, program products, team building, networking, influence, advocacy, time management, work and life balance
- Review of program documentation and completion of forms
- Review of time line
- Design of relationship time line in general
- Relationship consensus on goals and outcomes
- Handling conflict situations, and what to do "when the mentorship goes wrong"

Mentorship program content or curriculum can be delivered or made available through events, diverse modes and methods of communication, individual mentor and mentee activities, and activities for others in the program both specifically and in general. Specific examples include the following.

## EVENTS

- Recruitment meetings or receptions
- Presentation on program goals during organizational business meetings
- Presentations on program goals during an organization's staff development activities
- Orientation session for mentorship program participants
- Mentor orientation
- Mentor training sessions
- Mentee orientation
- Mentee training sessions
- Training sessions for all others involved specifically or tangentially in the program
- Evaluation activities
- Recognition activities
- Closure activities

## DIVERSE MODES AND METHODS OF COMMUNICATION

- Webinars
- Meetings (synchronous or asynchronous)
- Cloud products for storage of and access to documents or content
- Project work spaces such as wikis for sharing curriculum and projects; blogs for journaling about experiences, advising sessions, and for post-training and orientation discussions; team work space; project tracking work space
- Media streaming environments to house video and podcast streams for content delivery, teaching and learning, archived program activities, advising sessions
- E-mail as general correspondence
- E-mail as group threaded discussions
- Web page packages for backdrops for individual or group mentee projects
- Online calendars for posting time lines and processes or individuals or teams
- Online pictures for team building and post-event learning activity photo sharing, chronicling conversations, meetings, and so on
- Course management software to teach a class or cohort of learners with posting, discussion, pushing out notifications, and so on
- Online guides or paths used to post content for reading assignments or for creating forums for online projects
- Online survey environments to assist program planners in assessing and evaluating program elements, participants, and others involved either actively or tangentially

## ORIENTATION

Within the mentorship program, the orientation event provides some of the most critically important steps that ensure a foundation for the establishment and maintenance of a successful relationship. Orientation is a process designed to acclimate or introduce employees or workers to the basic elements of the workplace or department or their roles and responsibilities. It consists of the following, organized by timing.

### First Day

Information is provided on the physical setting for mentorship activities such as desk/office, communication tools, protocols and access, guidelines and rules for the locale, related employees and library workers, and required forms needing timely completion. In addition, if the mentee is being mentored for a specific position or level, he or she needs organizational content specific to this position such as the position job description, general roles and responsibilities, evaluation forms and time lines, workplace calendars, and the calendar for additional orientation time lines.

### First Week

Orientation for the first week includes the curriculum for the mentee process, curriculum of position roles and responsibilities, optional forms needing completion, introduction to peers and other related departments, mentorship process time lines, mentor time lines, mentorship protocols for communication, organizational communication and any nuances for mentorship communication, and the first stages of orientating the employee/mentee to position roles and responsibilities, as well as training time lines for both the mentorship relationship and the full training schedule.

### First Month

Orientation for the first month includes location information for adjacent and related areas, meeting all organizational managers, initial discussions or first meetings on curriculum for the mentee process, review of all required and optional forms completion discussion, and introduction to all organizational employees and workers. The first month orientation also includes first discussions on mentorship process time lines, review of communications distributed to date for roles and responsibilities, review of communications for mentorship processes, first steps for meeting with other mentees in the organization or in the mentorship program, and review of relevant organizational and management documents as well as review of reportage and communication due within the first month and immediately thereafter. During the first month, orientation will also occur with any clientele as well as any external individuals such as vendors, subcontractors, and employees from institutional partnerships. Additional "first month" orientation activities can include those based on the type and size of library as well as location—those co-locating or adjacent to the mentee work location, related support services such as neighborhood police, community outreach coordinators, technology departments, shared-space managers/employees, governing board members, advisory board members, as well as—for those very new to the area—locale or roles and responsibilities, and relevant association individuals.

Although orientation activities will vary given the type and size of organization, *the more important activities required* for orientations for the first week and first month for both the mentor and mentee include:

- content on the vision, mission, goals and outcomes of mentorship programs in general and specifically the organization's mentorship program;
- activities and exercises designed to establish initial connections for relationships;
- processes providing opportunities for mentors and mentees (and others involved) to learn about each other;
- overview of mentoring agreement, as well as a session for mentor and mentees to begin work on a mentoring action plan;
- review of roles, responsibilities, and expectations;
- data-gathering and discussion on content gathered in the application and selection process regarding mentor and mentee education and training needs;
- data-gathering and discussion on content gathered in the application and selection process regarding other individuals in the organization involved either generally or specifically;
- review of program time lines; and
- first week, first month, first three month activities.

# THE HANDBOOK AND ASSOCIATED CONTENT

Within the mentorship program, the instruction guide or handbook is the cornerstone of the curriculum. While the guide itself does *not* need to have all of the content, it should be online and include either content or links to content.

General content you can draw from outside your organization:

- the profession and professionalism (tenets of being a professional, ethical codes, standards);
- mentorship as a process;
- learning styles and teaching styles—general;
- first-year experience as an employee, career development, work patterns, work styles, productivity, program products, team building, networking, influence, advocacy, time management, work and life balance;
- handling conflict situations, or what to do "when the mentorship goes wrong";
- on communication (including modes and methods as well as techniques of communication);
- data-gathering support for evaluation; and
- making data-driven decisions about mentorship initiatives.

Content specific to your organization:

- to establish context for the type and size of library;
- for the organization hosting the program;
- on organizations that are active partners in the program;
- on the mentorship program of the institution (vision, mission, values, outcomes, rules and regulations);
- on the roles and responsibilities of mentors (goals and outcomes including listening skills, empathy, general and specific knowledge base on mentee needs, as well as communication skills and leadership, pedagogical, technology);
- on the roles and responsibilities of mentees (goals and outcomes);

- on the match and individual profiles of those in the match;
- on the learning and teaching styles of the mentors and mentees in the program;
- on the communication infrastructure of the organization's program;
- documentation;
- forms;
- a review of time line;
- the design of the relationship time line in general;
- relationship consensus on goals and outcomes; and
- relationship data gathering.

### • SCENARIO •

## A MENTEE QUESTION

We are moving a head of technical services librarian to a public services reference position and we are picking a mentor for him. We know he needs public service orientation and training. Does he need training to be a mentee?

*Yes!* Mentees can and do include new employees to the organization; existing employees who stay within their roles and responsibilities and are taking on additional roles and responsibilities; existing employees who are *not* staying within their roles and responsibilities but are taking on new roles and responsibilities (permanently); as well as existing employees who are *not* staying within their roles and responsibilities but are taking on new roles and responsibilities (temporarily). An additional category that could be considered a grey area is those employees who are *not* new to the organization but—in moving location or venue as well as roles and responsibilities—are new to the locale, and managers, employees, and workers as well as clientele in the new locale.

Clearly, this employee—who is taking on new roles and responsibilities permanently—has this issue as well as a variety of issues that require not only the more typical mentorship relationship but also other roles and responsibilities including:

- moving from one content area of focus to another or, in this case, moving from technical services to reference;
- changing departmental mission or support service to public service;
- changing from one challenging and frequently changing area (technical services) to another challenging and frequently changing area (reference);
- expanding communication focus with more public or customer service communication skills needed;
- downsizing from a management position (those in technical services) to a non-managerial position;
- reviewing knowledge base and skill sets for refreshing and expanding the use and application of reference resources;
- reviewing knowledge base and skills set for refreshing and expanding point-of-use information literacy roles and responsibilities; and
- reviewing knowledge base and skill sets for classroom instruction (examples: pedagogy, classroom management, teaching and learning styles).

No matter the category or type of mentee, all mentees need orientation, training, education, and development content and processes. Orientation does exactly *that*: the mentee receives orientation to the organization as experienced in the department or in specific roles and responsibilities. Depending on the category of the mentee, situation orienting can be first day, first week, or first month. Additional time lines for orientation might exist if—for example—the roles and responsibilities of the position don't occur until later in the year within the organization.

## CLEAR COMMUNICATIONS
## ORGANIZATION-WIDE

In addition, depending on both the organization and the mentorship/mentee processes, employees and workers—including those working directly with or for the mentor or the mentee as well as others in the organization—need specific orientations of their own to clarify:

- what mentee activities are;
- how mentee activities differ from that individual's position roles and responsibilities (examples: through "job" descriptions, paradigm shifts, and so on);
- mentee time lines as they affect others not involved in the process;
- what mentor activities are;
- how mentor roles and responsibilities differ from that individual's roles and responsibilities (examples: through job descriptions, paradigm shifts, and so on);
- mentor time lines as they affect others not involved in the process;
- roles and responsibilities of any employees or workers within the mentorship process; and
- mentorship time lines within the organization (if they differ from mentor/mentee activity time lines).

# 6

# MENTOR AND MENTEE ISSUES

## • A MENTOR CASE METHOD •

Dr. Flowers was surprised to see Burt Bentner's e-mail with a request for a letter of recommendation for a high-level position within a neighboring institution. His surprise stemmed from his concern that although he and Burt had had a very successful mentor/mentee relationship two years ago, Flowers did not think Burt was either ready or appropriate for the position he was applying for.

Flowers—not wanting to offend Burt, end their collegial relationship, steer him wrong for the request at hand, or risk recommending someone who would not be successful—replied to Burt that he needed a position description, an updated vita, and a rationale for his application for the new position *before* writing a recommendation.

Burt—offended by Flowers's e-mail reply—replied to Flowers that he was surprised Flowers needed this information about him since they had had such a successful mentor/mentee process and had remained friendly colleagues for the past two years. Burt also noted that Flowers and he were in the same organization and he should still be familiar with Burt's work.

What's wrong with this picture? How did they get to this point and how should things have occurred to avoid this situation? How should Flowers have handled it? How should Burt have handled it? Since they didn't handle it well, how should things be handled now?

The mentor's and mentee's expectations for post-mentorship activities might be unclear.

Post-mentorship communication—although not required—seems to be warranted in this case since a recommendation for Burt seems to be based on Flowers's knowledge of Burt *from* the mentorship.

Burt has provided very little information with the initial request. He should have remembered the protocol from mentorship orientation—specifically closure—and forwarded those documents (examples: job description, updated vita, and rationale) along with the request.

Although we don't have the wording of Flowers's reply, since Burt is offended, Burt should speak up and ask for clarity and rationale, given his perception of their relationship and his more informal approach to seeking assistance from a previous mentor.

Flowers should clarify the remarks he made and illustrate how a better request and a better use of his time would be to not only write the reference but to write it in the context of the previous relationship and the future position sought.

Flowers should check the mentorship instruction guide or handbook to see if this situation is covered and how it is covered. If the content isn't clear, he should inform the mentorship council of revisions or clarifications needed.

Flowers should review the instruction guide or handbook for the section on "handling conflict situations" or what to do "when the mentorship goes wrong."

## A MENTOR QUESTION

It can't all be good! Are there ever any problems with mentor/ mentee programs? What's the worst that could happen?

There is no promise that it will all be good. There *can* be problems with programs, mentors, and mentees. And the worst that can happen can include:

- mentees not being successful as mentees—that is, specific mentee activities either don't happen or don't happen fully;
- mentors not being successful as mentors—that is, specific mentor activities either don't happen or don't happen fully;
- mentor or mentee issues have a negative impact on a mentor's or mentee's primary positions within the organization;
- negative issues arise among others in the organization such as other non-mentees having problems with mentees;
- mentors and mentees part ways either during or after the relationship; and
- mentors and/or mentees leave the organization either during or after the relationship.

The following big picture and more specific issues are considered common program problems and contribute to answering the question "why might these things happen?"

# COMMON PITFALLS OF MENTORSHIP PROGRAMS

Big picture issues:

- No articulated program.
- Nothing is special or unique about the program.
- Program manager has no commitment, passion, or vision of mentorship.

- Inadequate personnel and/or resources to run the mentoring program.
- Lack of monitoring throughout mentor processes overall.
- Program staff has only superficial contact with its mentors and/or mentees.
- Vision, mission, goals, and values are not integrated at all or into critical parts of the program.
- A badly designed program for size, type, and so on of the institution or organization.
- A best practice program but not a good match for the size, type, and so on of the institution or organization.
- The rationale for the program is flawed, such as a program goal or outcome that focuses on succession planning but activities do not match succession planning.
- Not enough process in programs such as few forms, lack of organization, and so on.
- Curriculum confusion such as instruction on leadership and management is confused, or individual projects are not articulated.
- Lack of program training for mentors and/or mentees.
- No or little design of communication (example: for both good and bad news).
- Inadequate or unrealistic time lines such as too general, too specific, or no or poor match to organizational time lines.
- Lack of partnering and/or networking within the community.
- Little or no evaluation or poorly designed evaluation activities such as no, few, or non-specific outcomes.
- Evaluation wasn't conducted in a timely enough fashion to catch and correct issues or problems.

More specific issues:

- No criteria for matching mentors/mentees (examples: how individuals learn, existing skill set vs. required skill set for technologically driven mentorship activities).
- The mentor is not suited to mentorship.
- The mentee is not suited to menteeship.

- The wrong mentor/mentee match.
- Lack of orientation or "beginning" activities or processes.
- Lack of "post," ending, or closure activities or processes.
- Forms are present but are too general and are non-specific.
- Processes are used to substitute for activities that might be delivered better in a different way such as group or individual staff development or orientation to primary job responsibilities.
- Unclear expectations of mentees (example: the incorrect assumption that post-mentor activities should include support by the mentor for *all* of the mentee's endeavors such as all of their work within the organization or any positions they seek outside the organization).
- Unclear expectations of mentors.
- Lack of support by other employees not involved in the mentor process.
- Unclear, unarticulated, unexplained, nonexistent benefits for the mentor.
- Unclear, unarticulated, unexplained, nonexistent benefits for the mentee.
- Lack of mechanisms needed to support program activities, such as tracking, monitoring, and evaluation; and no, little, or inappropriate record-keeping during the process by all (examples: no diaries, no goals or outcomes articulated, no tracking of goals or outcomes, and so on).
- Incorrect program goals or outcomes such as the use of mentoring as a means to improve individual primary job performance.

The reality is that no matter how perfect the program is and no matter how perfect the mentor or how many past successes there have been, problems should be expected and are normal. Those managing the programs can anticipate issues; everyone knows that human error or personalities change within organizations, and change within individuals' lives can alter the course of the best-designed program. To reduce the likelihood of problems, however, a few general recommendations can help in this regard. Specifically, program designers should:

- design a program guide or handbook;
- create and communicate structure;
- evaluate, evaluate, and evaluate;
- create measurable, agreed-upon goals and outcomes;
- monitor relationship progress *throughout* the program and not wait too long or until a problem arises or until the "end" of the relationship;
- integrate a variety of evaluative, proactive, structural approaches instead of only asking mentors and mentees "how is it going?" questions (examples: observation, identified feedback, anonymous feedback, activity assessment such as deadlines met?, outcomes met?, and so on); and
- create proactive alternative plans to use if problems are identified (examples: standby mentors, outside conflict resolution participants).

And of course some issues that exist or occur are no one's fault, such as mentors or mentees not being at the right place in their career for the program or relationship; the organization or climate has changed and these activities are no longer possible, or the original goals of the program are no longer goals of the organization; or the personalities or work styles of the individuals involved are not or are no longer suited to the mentorship process or to each other.

Should these issues stop an organization from implementing a mentoring program? Obviously the answer is "no" with the realization that the benefits should and typically do outweigh negative aspects. And although recommendations for a successful program are integrated throughout this book, basic recommendations include how organizations—no matter how big or how small—should design a program that is the best match. A mentoring program should have a distinct process, forms, and so on; programs should have a significant communication component; programs should include an assessment and evaluative component; and individuals in the program should be vetted and matched.

Finally, some issues arise that are outside the bounds of any appropriate behavior in a mentorship program. Program planners should be aware of these possible situations and be ready to respond by—if necessary—stopping mentorship activities overall or switching relationship participants. These can be articulated in three categories—inappropriate direction or activity, bad mentors, and bad mentees.

## INAPPROPRIATE DIRECTION OR ACTIVITIES

### Counseling for Personal Issues

Because of many reasons—federal health legislation or institutional guidelines notwithstanding—it's often hard to detect when either mentors or mentees need special assistance such as physical, emotional, or mental assistance. The reality is that this can happen in the mentorship relationship. This doesn't mean that someone with physical, emotional, or mental problems will always bring them into the mentorship relationship; however, if the problems do become part of the discussion, all parties should immediately seek a third party to initiate a referral for either party. And while it's not always clear when it does happen, either party if suspecting, should signal a "time out" of the discussion or exchange and put a hiatus on the mentorship activities until questions are answered or issues are clarified.

Program planners should consider program training to include balancing the work life or wellness discussions with the more "difficult discussions" as well as referral content to assist participants in recognizing and dealing with these situations.

### Personal Relationships

Sometimes it's not possible to stop or ignore personal relationships from forming whether they are wanted or unwanted. Not only should mentors and mentees pause the relationship to share the issue with the program planners, but observers who suspect that a more personal relationship is forming—whether wanted or unwanted—should immediately report the situation. These issues should be referred to in mentorship instruction guides or handbooks as well.

### Confidentiality Breached

Information and content shared during mentorship activities might be sensitive for participants or others in the organization. The expectation of those involved in the program is that—within the communication guidelines—confidentiality requirements are articulated. In addition, standards for confidentiality should be clearly addressed and adhered to for both written and verbal communications as well as behaviors within the process.

## BAD MENTORS

Beyond the more common failures in relationships such as a failure due to lack of contact by the mentor or lack of focus on the needs of the mentee, there are mentor failures that should be articulated in the instruction guide or handbook and addressed in mentor training. And while many can't believe that mentors might have hidden agendas or ulterior motives, the reality is that bad mentors do exist.

### Unhappy at Work

Every organization has employees who are unhappy at work. While it is an individual's own business whether or not they are happy at work and why they might be unhappy at work, mentors should be individuals who—no matter how they feel—can keep personal or professional unhappiness out of the mentor/mentee relationship. Mentorship coordinators can add screening questions to application forms and interview questions as well as add curricula that address the importance of what might and might not be shared within the program. If individuals are determined to be unhappy, bitter, or angry, it should be addressed within the training to see if mentors can avoid these discussions. If they can, then mentors should stay within the program. If program coordinators determine that potential mentors cannot separate issues, then they should not be considered for mentoring relationships at the time of assessment. Program coordinators should not, however, permanently exclude individuals who might otherwise be successful mentors. Rather, they should work with individuals to find ways to separate out negative from positive approaches to sharing information. Changing the mind of someone who is unhappy at work is not the job of the mentorship program. What makes them unhappy is typically not the concern of the mentorship team.

## Disinterested

Some mentors may start out interested and become disinterested or begin disinterested (for whatever the reason) and want nothing to do with the assignment for the duration of the assignment. No matter what the reason, mentors not wishing to participate or participate only minimally should not accept or continue in the mentoring assignment for many reasons. For example, disinterest is often more damaging to mentees than bad mentoring; disinterest is often hard to detect in a timely fashion; and, it's often hard to decide when to report the situation and/or leave the relationship. Also, while other problems or issues might be able to be fixed, apathy is often hard to "cure" or change. If program coordinators want to attempt to change the "disinterested" mentor, motivational training is recommended.

## Know-It-All

It's not unusual for mentors to be chosen because they know more than others and sometimes they do, in fact, know more than others in the organization in certain or even many areas. Therefore it's hard to weigh appropriate levels of knowledge and self-confidence versus inappropriate levels of knowledge and self-confidence. This category of mentor, however, is typically someone who acts as if they know more than others but in actuality know less or nothing at all. Program coordinators should take care to sort out this group of interested but unacceptable mentors. Recommendations for how to do that include requiring references with applications from peers rather than only supervisors; requiring statements for applications that include measures of knowledge through posing questions for answers, or seeking general statements of purpose or knowledge.

## Self-Serving

Often called opportunists, self-serving individuals seek appointments or service in order to enhance their reputation or career at the expense of others. While professionals do not want to consider that these individuals might be more than self-serving, and are actually overtly destructive to the careers of others, planners should not rule out the possibility. Identifying ways to alter the behavior of self-serving individuals includes requiring references from peers rather than only supervisors, carefully vetting mentor goals, and carefully assigning mentees to mentors.

### Inappropriate Claim

Mentors seeking an inordinate amount of gratitude, glory, or responsibility for the success of the mentorship relationship or mentee make inappropriate claims on the mentorship program. Seeking extraordinary acclaim often comes with the mentor not doing a fair share of the work or doing less then expected or needed. Similar to the self-serving mentor, the mentor's initial commitment or interest in the program or service is hyperbole. Individuals with this approach are particularly destructive in a program that seeks to uplift others by sharing knowledge and teaching others. Similar to the self-serving approach, recommendations for effecting change include requiring references from peers rather than only supervisors and carefully vetting mentor goals.

### Outside the Box

Some mentors are considered exemplary because they stand out, think differently, or have expansive personalities. Some, however, think outside the more typically organizational "boxes" and as such do not "follow the rules." While these mentors are not always inappropriate in that role, care should be taken to ensure that they understand they are working to assist in an assimilation or planned growth process, rather than a process to get others to join processes outside organizational directions. Recommendations for effecting change include pre-drafting goals for mentors that are acceptable to the organization, pre-selecting projects for mentors and mentees to choose from, and including mentors in the curriculum design.

Other characteristics of bad mentors include their being bossy, ill-prepared, bitter, or disrespectful. No matter the characteristic, mentorship program planners should design and require in-depth application processes, plan and execute extensive mentor training, consider mentor coordinators, seek best practices from similar institutions, and integrate reward and recognition processes into their mentorship programs.

## BAD MENTEES

While fully developed mentorship programs are typically volunteer in nature, aspects of them—such as orientation for new employees—can be required. In addition, it is not uncommon for new professionals to be assigned a first-year mentor who can assist them in navigating the environment or to guide them in significant roles and responsibilities such as research and writing for promotion and tenure. Mentees in mentorship programs are, however, typically not *required* to apply to be mentees; rather, full mentorship programs are intended to enhance existing work at the point in an employee's career when it can be most meaningful.

No matter the reason, "bad" mentee situations can lead to mentees feeling that they are required to participate in a program that is—rather than helpful—merely more work. Individuals who are accepted to programs may feel that the program or attention makes it all "about them." Mentees might react negatively to the program due to a bad match with mentors, or to a match with a bad mentor. Mentees may willfully choose to cause trouble in the program by lack of participation or contributing only through group negativity. There are mentees who feel they know more than any others do and do not honor individual or group expertise, and there are mentees who choose not to follow the rules and regulations or group processes.

Recommendations to avoid bad mentees include the design and communication of clear management expectations for mentees in the program; clear mentorship program goals; pre-drafted mentee goals for mentors and mentees to choose from; and relationship project lists approved prior to relationships.

Finally, problems in mentorship programs will also come when employees not involved in the program are unhappy with the process. To that end, the mentorship program should include work with professionals not in the program as well as other employees and workers who need information on the process and the time lines as well as how the mentorship process relates to them. Examples of how they might relate to the process include:

- providing both primary- and secondary-level information on the nature of their own roles and responsibilities regarding the mentorship program within the organization;
- outline of time lines for the mentoring process for the organization, for the department, as well as clarification of the beginning and end of the process in general;
- outline of mentee times of availability and unavailability during the mentorship process (beginning, end, during a workday, during a workweek);
- alerts to activities that may affect their own work such as a period of time when there might be more questions asked of them relating to their own primary and secondary job responsibilities;
- any changes to standard communication protocols during the mentee time period; and
- role in feedback (to the mentor or the mentorship process) and—as appropriate—evaluation of the mentee.

# BEST PRACTICES FOR MENTORSHIP PROGRAM MEASUREMENT AND EVALUATION

**I**N ORDER TO survive and grow, an organization must measure and evaluate success. Building a culture of assessment, however, is a combination of not only valuing measurement and evaluation but also committing to a culture of assessment that strives to ask the "why" and design the "how" in order to create data to drive decision making. These data come from external and internal sources and are used to measure achievement and success of existing areas of the organization as well as to design new programs. Measurement and assessment data include data gathered from external environments used for comparisons in general or specific areas, best practices data determined externally, best practices data determined by the organization itself, internal data gathered due to an organization's commitment to measurement and evaluation, and gathering data to illustrate use and accountability and compete for funding dollars. In addition, data is also gathered for a "higher purpose," including to contribute to data sets for federal, state, regional, and local government and other organizations; to meet standards at a variety of levels; to contribute to association initiatives; for crafting legislative messages; and to contribute to vendor or commercial initiatives. Even with all these opportunities for gathering and using data, however, the reality is that some data goes unassessed or unused, and—of specific importance—some data can be used for more than one initiative. Thus, program planners of expanded or new initiatives should always begin planning by determining what measurement and evaluation data is available in related professions as well as in the library profession; what data does the organization have already in place; and—most importantly—whether or not using or reusing the data could contribute to any program goals for short-term or long-term "longitudinal" evaluation. In addition, richer measurement and evaluation comes from not only gathering and using flat or one-dimensional data but from focusing on gathering data to create multileveled data. And although the majority of professionals are not statisticians and although much data can't be the only determining factor in success nor the final or causal predictor, data *can* be used for evidence of need and affect as well as success in achieving goals and measuring outcomes.

## GENERAL TIPS

So, with a general stance that mentorship programs cannot be successful either in the short term or long term without measurement and evaluation, program planners should:

- create goals, strategies, and outcomes for their mentorship program in general;
- decide what data results matter for measuring achievement of program goals, strategies, and outcomes;
- review what measurements are already in place in the organization that are appropriate for use in the program; and
- decide what and how measurements need to be put in place overall to measure the success of program goals and outcomes.

Once general measurement approaches have been discussed, planners need to review all program aspects to decide:

- Given organizational measurement, what data can be used specifically for the program?

- Based on general program goals, what additional measurement must be put in place?
- Based on general mentor goals, what measurement must be put in place?
- Based on general mentee goals, what measurement must be put in place?

## APPLYING EXISTING MEASUREMENTS TO THE MENTORSHIP PROGRAM

Although libraries typically don't measure "too much" or even in all aspects of the library, there are types and styles of measurement that libraries are already using that can contribute data—on its own or linked with a new measurement—to contribute to program success. Examples of what and how include:

| EXISTING MEASUREMENTS | HOW MEASUREMENTS MIGHT BE USED FOR MENTORSHIP PROGRAM MEASUREMENT |
| --- | --- |
| Organizational culture assessments | Management and employee existing survey questions on presence of a culture of teaching and learning, value of professional development, opportunities for advancement, value of individual growth |
| Individual or departmental job satisfaction surveys | Employee satisfaction with the organization, likelihood of advancement possible, agreement of development opportunities—number and type overall, agreement of development opportunities—number and type overall specific to individual positions |
| Staff development surveys of awareness, need, and satisfaction | Employee satisfaction with dollars available for professional development for individuals; satisfaction with dollars available for professional development for areas or departments; opinions on presence of basic vs. in-depth or advanced development opportunities; agreement of development opportunities—number and type overall, agreement of development opportunities—number and type overall specific to individual positions; availability and support for training; availability and support for education |

*(continued)*

| | |
|---|---|
| **Committee or team leadership availability** | Individuals volunteer for committee, team service; individuals volunteer for committee, team projects; individuals volunteer for/apply for committee, team leadership; individuals' service and success rate on numbers of committees and teams |
| **Organizational goals and outcomes** | Management focus on and growth of employees through professional development, and so on; goals, outcomes for completing development, training and education; outcomes for organizational leadership and management in general and on committees and teams |
| **Departmental goals and outcomes** | Presence of cross-trained employees; growth in competencies in basic and advanced areas; implementation success when, for example, new knowledges are required |
| **Human resources data such as employee turnover, length of time in employment, exit interviews, number of applications to posted positions** | Organizational data on retention of employees; internal applications for new and existing positions; overall years of service; satisfaction with the organization in exit interviews; reason for leaving the organization in exit interviews; percentage of job offers vs. jobs filled |
| **Employee evaluation growth such as increased success in specific areas; changes in evidence of accomplishment in, for example, portfolios** | Employee evaluations indicate positive performance; growth in performance excellence; organizational productivity |
| **Employee accomplishment such as promotion; tenure** | Employee reportage indicate evidence of growth through achievements of organization success such as promotion, tenure; employee reportage of achievements such as awards, degrees, certificates |

# MEASURES SPECIFIC TO MENTORSHIP

| PROGRAM GOALS | MEASURING PROGRAM GOALS |
| --- | --- |
| **Grow the organization's own into leaders and managers** | Pre-self-assessment of numbers of and skill sets of existing managers; survey of interest levels of entry-level professionals; focus group of new professionals who have completed one management or leadership project |
| **Increase opportunities for professional development** | Count the number and type of opportunities over the last [number] years; survey attendees or completers to determine use and application of information; share ideas from all professionals through an e-mail threaded discussion; post a draft of proposed professional development curriculum and invite comments through blog postings; gather suggestions of existing models of organizational professional development on the internal wiki and gather feedback from employees through online surveys |
| **Expand individual ownership of workplace projects** | Ask for a review of the past [number] years of annual organization and departmental reports and solicit additional projects begun but not completed, still needed, and completed; survey managers for names of individual project leaders and managers and completers; seek group feedback through individual interview schedules with project managers and leaders |
| **Re-energize a middle-level manager, leader cohort** | Survey middle-level manager, leader cohort on satisfaction with management and leadership activities, organization commitment to professional development, individual job satisfaction as managers and leaders; schedule focus group with entry-level professionals on individual plans for roles and responsibilities and comparison with data from entry-level focus group participants |
| **Energize entry-level professionals** | Survey entry-level professionals on awareness of and satisfaction with management and leadership activities, organization commitment to professional development, individual job satisfaction; schedule focus group with entry-level professional to determine individual plans for roles and responsibilities expanding into management and leadership |

# CHOOSE RIGHT-FIT OPTIONS

Mentorship program planners should take care to choose evaluation mechanisms that fit needs; examples include:

- *Tests* (pre and post). Tests serve a variety of purposes and are excellent evaluation mechanisms for planning and comparison data. They can be print or online or both, and can not only gather data and opinion but also educate, change an attitude, and gain awareness of the situation at hand for the organization, and inform individuals and increase individual self-awareness. Standardized tests can also be designed to assess and demonstrate levels of knowledge and levels of skills and abilities. Mentors' and mentees' initial levels of competencies should be tested for comparison data, illustration of growth, self-awareness of program participants, and so on.
- *Questionnaires/surveys.* Surveys are common evaluation instruments, and with the advent of online environments of vetted surveys as well as free or low-cost online, easy-to-design-and-deliver software, extensive general data can be gathered, as well as specific data for attitude assessment, levels of satisfaction, gathering opinion, and assessment of institutionally specific assessment of competencies. Surveys—like tests—are also excellent mechanisms for gathering comparison data.
- *Interviews.* Although group discussions are valuable, individual discussions are also valuable as both initial as well as follow-up or comparison methods of eliciting information. Interviews can be open-ended discussions or can have interview schedules of scripted questions. Interviews scheduled both before, during, and after activities can be used for comparison of information, as well as gathering more sensitive feedback. These processes can be used to determine behavior and attitudinal changes.
- *Focus groups.* Focus groups are an evaluation mechanism that provide multileveled opportunities to gather ideas, present information, and gather opinions, discuss disparate

ideas or gather information from like-minded people, build consensus or gain support for varieties of ideas, and finally, network within an environment or cohort. Using facilitators—either internal or external to the organization or within the organization but external to the process—focus group processes can include scripted questions for general or invited audience feedback, content presented to gain awareness, and content gathered and "voted" on to illustrate consensus or the lack thereof.

- *Blogs, journals.* Introspective forums are for sharing information or posting. Blogs or journals assist coordinators in helping participants share opinions and self-expression, share expertise, offer opinions, and use experiences to illustrate ideas. And as with other online resources, the strength of these resources provides additional complexities with their synchronous as well as asynchronous availability of content, as well as for providing opportunities for others in an activity or program to weigh in at the point of discussion or after.

Evaluating mentorship activities also includes evaluating any products or projects completed by mentors or mentees. Although these evaluations should use the organization's standards or rubrics for success as well as outcomes identified from goals, mentorship products should also be reviewed for levels of completeness, whether they meet the *original* intent of the product, whether they were completed according to planning time lines, whether the original or intended individuals were responsible, and whether the product achieves success according to mentorship program goals.

## WHAT THE DATA IS TELLING US

Finally, when reviewing the professional literature of mentorship, evaluation data provides program recommendations.

- Participants are more satisfied and gained more from the program when the organization of activities, meetings, goal development, and mentor and mentee contact were more structured at the beginning of the process. Examples include guidelines for specific contacts at the beginning of the conference or within an institution within the first two weeks of the relationship that should be directive as to time and day and include activities. (Example: mentees should send an e-mail within the first forty-eight hours of the mentor/mentee program with "profile" questions answered and the title or link to the "professional content that they refer to the most in their job." Mentors should respond within the first work week with their "profile" elements and the "professional material they most recommend for their mentee" to review prior to the second mentee contact.)

- Mentor and mentee matching processes should strive for comparable levels of technological expertise (length and type of experience as well as ease of use with communication opportunities).

- Although more contacts and activities should occur at the onset of the relationship, relationship time lines should include specific structure for contacts between or among mentors and mentees within the first thirty days of the relationship (day of the week, time of day, length of time for discussion/meeting, and so on) *and* should outline—no matter what the frequency—connections throughout the life of the relationship.

- Not all relationships will be the best match or will be completed; however, the more prepared the mentors and mentees and the greater the structure for the process, the greater the chance for success.

- Content should be introduced throughout the mentorship program; that is, although environments should be created to "house" or post content, not all content should be posted from day one of the program. This progressive accessing of content should also be for activities, exercises, project or product information, and basic curriculum.

- Program exercises should be directed to participants to work separately as well as together either in assessment or comparison. In addition, active learning pedagogies should be used (cases, simulations) to have mentors and mentees approaching issues and problems together and discussing solutions.

- Introductory program content should include recognizable signposts and signals for relationships with problems. Specific measures of issues and challenges to success should be shared early on for intervention.
- Programs with branding, slogans, and logos should also have extras such as unique curriculum, unique opportunities for feedback, events and activities, celebrations, and recognition.

# APPENDIXES

**A**PPENDIXES ARE ADDITIONAL information located at the end of a report or other monograph. As supplementary materials they are designed to illustrate monograph content by providing examples for information previously introduced. Although it isn't the case for all monograph content, the literature on mentoring offers a wide variety of forms, templates, and checklists recommended for organizations. These examples are for planning, before, during, and after mentorship program events and activities and each one has been revised or designed as—for the most part—Swiss cheese content (example: blanks, holes, and empty boxes) so that organizations can more easily personalize content for their own programs and initiatives.

## General Guidelines for Content

- Forms, templates, and checklists are critical aspects of programs no matter what the type or size of the organization.
- Information must be maintained in print and online in multiple locations initially until the organization has finalized all documents throughout a pilot program, then online environments must be carefully organized and maintained.
- Sample completed forms, templates, and checklists with rubrics for measuring appropriateness of completed content should be maintained by the organization.

General Recommendations (using "form" but meaning "forms, templates and checklists"):

- Make sure you have "all the forms you need."
- To track what is needed, create a master form/checklist of forms needed.
- Arrange master checklists by the planning, before, during, and after stages of the program.
- Use standardized subject headings; reviewed and revised time lines; and legends identifying authorship and distribution.
- All forms must be placed on a strict review and revision schedule that must be adhered to with organizations. This schedule needs to include a review of the primary organization's forms as well as review time lines from related partners and ancillary organizations.
  1. Form content must:
     a. Remain current
     b. Reflect new issues
     c. Indicate different needs unique to evolving relationships
     d. Indicate new/changing resources such as communication software
     e. Include general organizational changes such as shifting functions, new titles, new job descriptions
     f. Include collaboration issues and changes such as expanded or different community partners
  2. Forms should avoid colloquialisms, "insider" references, initialisms, acronyms, and references to "who does what" by name of individual rather than by title for the greatest, easiest level of comprehension. Individuals reading and using forms should not have to "guess" what something means.
  3. Forms must be replicated in look or branding across program content, and online content should be in PDF form to expand possibilities for exact duplication.
  4. Forms should include space for indicating (initials, codes, titles, and so on) who completes the form—and in some cases—indication of all who handled or used the form during the event.

5. Forms must have space for legends for explanation of abbreviations, signatures, or "sign-offs," titles, and so on, and meanings needed for in-house or unique information from the primary organization or partners.

6. Forms must be assessed to determine if multiple languages are needed on some or all forms.

7. Forms must be assessed to determine if graphics are needed to illustrate issues on all or some forms.

8. Forms should be designed for standard sizes of notebooks, and so on for ease of use, duplication, and distribution.

9. Online forms should be designed for web environments and assessed to determine if content is displayed as appropriate across web browsers; however, form design should also ensure content can be printed and used without need for revision or reformatting, and for ease of use, duplication, and distribution.

10. Form designs should avoid using elements that do not reproduce easily (colors or ink in general, multiple colors, and color of paper).

11. Form designs should avoid using elements that illustrate ideas but do not reproduce easily or at all (complicated charts, ideas defined by colors that don't duplicate or are too expensive to duplicate).

12. Forms should be designed to conform to green or sustainable organizational goals or commitments.

13. Gathering content on mentoring is both easy and difficult. That is:

    a. Although the concept of mentoring is both historical and classic, not all classic mentorship content is still applicable to contemporary situations or individuals. Older material may be exclusive of certain groups or may use incorrect or inappropriate terminology.

    b. Using a monograph to provide mentor content is difficult as the static nature of older monographs—unless digitized—may have outdated forms.

c. Using bibliographies and webographies from monographs, periodicals, and websites is standard practice, but because of the temporary or evolving nature of mentor programs, many links—including some identified as best practices—are old and not working.

d. Much of the content from mentorship programs can be duplicated for use in other environments.

# PROGRAM PLANNING

Any program that involves employees and library workers should be planned carefully and with great concern for everyone involved. To ensure mentor programs or even mentor pilots or "test runs" with only a few people involved requires a carefully planned and standardized planning process.

## Mentorship Program Planning Process

1. Identify the values, beliefs, or assumptions of the organization that relate to human resources to determine the role mentoring might play in the life of the organization for employees and workers. If a problem or issue has already been determined regarding human resources, articulate the problem or issue first and then identify the values, beliefs, or assumptions of the organization that relate problems or issues to human resources to determine the role mentoring might play.

2. Decide who will be the process owner for the mentoring initiative and its stages of design and implementation and create a team to design and implement the program.

3. Conduct an environmental scan: identify SWOT or strengths, weaknesses, opportunities, and threats and relevant benchmarks, and models to determine how mentoring can assist the organization in solving problems or addressing issues. Additional content needed by the process owner and the team includes:
   - financial issues for the plan including actual dollars and in-kind costs
   - profiles of those in the process including planners, mentors, mentees, others in the organization involved, and others in the organization not involved
   - data from the organization such as focus group content, management discussion, aggregated evaluation

content, human resources issues such as orientation issues, and professional development

- marketing information such as possible program branding
- need for and techniques to use in convincing the umbrella organization of the importance of the program to the organization
- plans for an advisory presence such as an advisory council
- related plans for partners, the organization's "community"
- history of related library initiatives, including successes and failures
- role of and opportunities for integrating a technology infrastructure into the initiative
- identification of other related programs or programs integrated into partners or, in the case of an institution, the presence of a similar program in a local, regional, or state association
- any related standards such as required institutional or organizational competencies in general as well as required competencies during an employee's probationary period, guidelines for tenure and promotion, and so on
- any human resources requirements related to the program such as overtime, and so on
- decisions for or against mandates such as when should the program be required
- benchmark program documents
- the organization's existing content to assess for needed review and revision.

4. Create vision and mission statements for mentoring for the organization.

5. Develop the roles, goals, and values of mentoring for the organization.

6. Develop objectives, strategies, outcomes, and a strategic plan for mentoring. This requires identifying resource funds and a review of any policies and procedures that need to be revised or need to be developed.

7. Implement the strategic plan.
8. Monitor, evaluate, and adjust the plan as goals and outcomes are accomplished.

## Mentorship Program Overview

1. Introduction
2. Team
3. Vision/Direction Goals, Outcomes, Strategies
4. Measurement and Accountability
5. Description—a Mentor
6. Description—a Mentee
7. Description—Advisory Council
8. Process
    - Time lines
    - Review and Design of Infrastructure (Policies, Procedures, and Processes)
    - Documentation including:
        i. Job Descriptions
        j. Benefits Statements
        k. Applications
9. Curriculum Plan
        j. Mentors
        k. Mentees
        l. Others (such as Advisory Council, Partnership roles and responsibilities)
13. Teaching and Learning Modes and Methods (Mentors, Mentees, Others)
14. Participant Profiles (including Advisory Council)
15. Communication Plan
16. Marketing Plan
17. Evaluation (Measurement, Accountability, Performance, Feedback)
18. Budget (dollars spent, in-kind)
19. Resources
20. Forms, Templates, Checklists

# JOB DESCRIPTIONS

## Mentorship Program Coordinator/Process Owner: Position Description

The mentoring program coordinator or process owner is appointed by the [title] and is responsible for the leadership and management of the mentorship program. This position reports directly to [name] and works in tandem with the human resources manager and the professional development team. The mentorship program is supported by an administrative assistant III and shares this position (50 percent) with the human resources department. The coordinator/process owner will manage seven areas of the mentorship experience, including the overall vision, mission, goals, and outcomes. Roles and responsibilities involve general management and oversight of processes and include:

1. Program Infrastructure Design and Delivery
    a. Participants
    b. Communication
    c. Documentation
2. Curriculum Design and Delivery
3. Budgeting/Fund-Raising
4. Education and Training
5. Marketing and Public Information
6. Records Management
7. Measurement and Evaluation

Specifically the coordinator will:
- Manage the mentorship processes including mentors and mentee activities based on the program's infrastructure, policies, and procedures
- Manage program mentors and mentees including application, matching, orientation, initial and ongoing training, goals, and outcomes

- Communicate effectively with employees and workers including marketing and public relations for maintaining and increasing awareness of the mentorship program and its benefits and value to the organization and its employees
- Work in collaboration with the primary mentorship audiences including the advisory council, mentors, and mentees
- Work in collaboration with the secondary mentorship audiences such as (internally) other employees indirectly involved in the program (orientation, training) and mentor and mentee supervisors; and (externally) the umbrella organization, partners, and stakeholders
- Oversee finance and budget activities
- Provide leadership to the organization regarding mentorship.

The coordinator/process owner serves in this role for no more than three years and has an evaluation (conducted by the x) specifically on his or her role apart from their organizational evaluation process.

## Advisory Council—Roles and Responsibilities

The advisory council is appointed through a process managed by the mentorship program coordinator/process owner and is responsible for assistance and support for the leadership and management of the mentorship program. The council is comprised of both internal and external representatives with a balance of managers, front-line employees, and individuals with varying degrees of experience within the profession and the organization.

The council assists in the overall deployment of the program but specifically with vetting content, participant selection, marketing and public relations and, as appropriate, fund-raising. Specifically, advisory council members will:

- Begin marketing the mentorship program, and advocate for support of the program
- Assist in design of a work plan for advisory group meetings
- Review draft content (need, purpose)
- Review draft content (job descriptions, budget, time lines, and so on)

- Work with coordinator/process owner to draft marketing and communication plans
- Work on design and implementation of the mentor and mentee content
- Serve on mentor and mentee interview/selection teams
- Work with teams to match participants
- Attend advisory group meetings and trainings as appropriate
- Evaluate progress on work plan for advisory group meetings
- Monitor progress of mentor/mentee relationships
- Vet data/evaluation
- Assess goal completion and success of outcomes
- Identify successes, failures of communication, and marketing plans
- Assist in the evaluation of the program coordinator
- Assist in the program annual report activities

## Mentor Program Participant Supervisor— Roles and Responsibilities

Mentor and mentee supervisors—although not active participants in the mentorship process—do have delineated roles in the program and should be active partners in the success of the program. Supervisors' roles and responsibilities for mentors and mentees include:

- Assess potential mentor or mentee performance to assist in the determination of availability for the mentor program
- Serve as a recommendation for possible participant
- Assist with completion of application as needed
- Vet goals and outcomes as appropriate
- Assist in discussion of association/organization membership and service
- Assist in design of time line as needed
- Assist in the determination of project, research or publication ideas, direction
- Provide constructive feedback as requested or appropriate
- Attend events as appropriate (examples: networking, training, and so on)

- Serve as a resource person for mentor/mentee activities as needed
- Assist in problem-solving as needed
- Assist in support of mentorship in general and in communication of benefit and value of mentoring
- Assist in communicating mentor content to employees not directly involved in the mentorship process
- Participate in program evaluation as needed

## Mentor Program Mentor: Position Description

Mentors provide expertise and support for (first-year professionals, employees moving to new departments, and so on) through the mentor program. This formal relationship is a (two-year, first year of employment, 18 month) commitment and is designed to orient, acculturate, and guide these individuals through their (first year of work, first two years of work, orientation and move to their new department) and in the design and development of a project, in the establishment of a research direction, and through (product design and completion, their first evaluation, publication.) In addition, mentors provide direction on association membership and service and foster opportunities for networking.

### MENTOR ROLES/RESPONSIBILITIES

- Serve as a guide and resource
- Provide a professional networking opportunity
- Design—in partnership with mentee—goals and outcomes
- Support the teaching and learning relationship through attendance at orientations, meetings, and trainings
- Support the match or relationship through attendance at regularly scheduled mentor/mentee events
- Follow communication plan
- Participate in measurement and evaluation

### MENTOR REQUIREMENTS/QUALIFICATIONS

- Commitment to the program or process
- Good communication skills

- Availability
- Match to mentee needs through competence in desired areas
- Skilled in teaching and presentation and discussion

## Mentor Program Mentee: Position Description

Mentees are defined as (any new employee who is in their first month of hire and seeks assistance in navigating their first six months or probationary period from someone other than their immediate supervisor, an employee moving to a new department, an employee moving to a new location, an employee promoted to different roles and responsibilities within their existing department or a new department). Relationships between mentees and mentors can be a one-to-one or two-to-three mentees who—as a team—seek assistance from a mentor. Pairings are for a minimum of six months and typically no more than one year and orients and acclimates the individual(s) to the organization or specific work area or responsibilities.

### MENTEE ROLES/RESPONSIBILITIES

- Establish needs and articulate overall goals with mentor
- Identify activities and time line—with the mentor—for attendance at orientations, meetings, and trainings
- Actively participate in the pairing through attendance at regularly scheduled mentor/mentee events
- Follow the agreed-upon communication plan
- Participate in measurement and evaluation

### MENTEE REQUIREMENTS/QUALIFICATIONS

- Commitment to the program/process
- Desire to learn and grow in the organization
- Desire for success during (their first year of work, their move to a new department, the first six months of employment)
- Availability

# Mentorship Program for the x Association

### PROCESS OWNER/ADVISORY COUNCIL CHAIR/TEAM LEADER

The process owner will manage the mentorship experience including the overall vision, mission, goals, and outcomes. Roles and responsibilities involve general management of processes including but not limited to budgeting, communication, and assessment. Specifically the (Process Owner, Chair, Team Leader, Coordinator) will:

- Manage the mentorship processes, including mentor and mentee activities based on the association's infrastructure, policies, and procedures
- Manage program mentors and mentees including application, matching, orientation, initial and ongoing training, meeting goals, and outcomes of relationships
- Coordinate association mentorship activities at annual conferences and business meetings
- Manage the mentor e-environment for communication, teaching, and learning infrastructure
- Communicate effectively with members, including public relations and marketing for maintaining and increasing awareness of the mentorship program and its benefits and values
- Work in collaboration with the primary mentorship audiences, including the association board, the membership advisory council, the teaching and learning cohort, mentors, and mentees
- Oversee annual budget activities
- Work in collaboration with the secondary mentorship audiences such as (internally) member libraries directly involved in the program (orientation, training) and mentor and mentee supervisors
- Provide leadership to the association for strategic planning and sustainability regarding mentorship.

# GOALS/OUTCOMES

Mentor programs must—like all other areas of libraries—be evaluated. Although organizations measure success in a variety of ways, mentorship programs should

- Have attainable goals ("Everyone is oriented to the institution after the first mentor/mentee session" is not an easily attainable goal based on "numbers" requested such as "everyone" and the nature of what would be a broad, vague definition of "oriented").
- Provide meaningful measurement for evaluation (meaningful results should move beyond "how many mentors signed up" or one-dimensional data).
- Use standardized measurements of the organization. (If the library uses strategies, the program should use strategies; if the grant supporting the project requires outcomes, the program should use outcomes.)

Mentor programs should have—at the very least—general program goals or outcomes as well as mentor and mentee goals or outcomes. Examples include:

## Program Goals

- To assess the organization's onboarding needs for all new employees
- To identify funding issues regarding the organization's two-day orientation requirement
- To determine benefits of the association's half-day "new member" conference training activities

## Program Outcomes

- New employees successfully completing the organization's acculturation webinar will indicate an "overall level of participant satisfaction" of 4 or greater on the webinar pre and post evaluation.
- "First day" employees will rate—on the webinar post-test—3 points higher than on the webinar's pre-test on "knowledge of management's first week expectations."
- Mentees exiting the first year mentorship program will indicate "high levels of satisfaction of a six or better on an eight point Likert Scale" with their mentor.
- Mentees exiting the first year mentorship program will indicate "high levels of satisfaction of a six or better on an eight-point Likert Scale" with the curriculum and training provided for mentees.

## Mentor Goals

- To contribute to the organization's first-year "transforming initiative" by serving as a mentor for a new employee in the [name of] department.
- To expand appreciative inquiry competencies for application in the organization's "buddy program."
- To participate in the association's "leadership in service" program by volunteering or applying to mentor two post-leadership week participants.

## Mentor Outcomes

- Mentors successfully completing the "leadership in service" program will serve as chair of an association task force.
- Mentors successfully completing the organization's on-boarding training will mentor two new employees in the first-year program.
- Mentors volunteering to support the "on-the-spot" mentor/mentee network will—after six months of service—also

apply for the "Integrating New Employees" mentor/mentee program.

## Mentee Goals

- To increase knowledge of the opportunities for advancement in the organization
- To identify like-minded employees for workplace networking for peer training in the organization's cutting-edge technology projects
- To complete the first year promotion and tenure checklist successfully by working with a research coach in the mentorship program

## Mentee Outcomes

- Mentees finishing their research initiative with their research coach will volunteer to serve on the "on-the-spot" research committee for one-year post-mentee activities to meet their first-year service requirement
- Mentees' completion of required self-paced new employee seminars will indicate higher levels of satisfaction (eight or greater on a ten-point Likert Scale) with understanding of their performance requirements
- Mentees seek assistance with at least two areas of career development planning from mentor career coaches throughout the first-year mentor program

# CHECKLISTS

## Program Checklist

PLANNING

- ❏ Identify need and match of mentor program to organizational need
- ❏ Obtain necessary approvals
- ❏ Begin marketing idea, advocating for support, participants
- ❏ Define and profile the mentee population
- ❏ Define and profile the mentor population
- ❏ Select the process owner
- ❏ Select and contact the advisory group
- ❏ Research best practices to match environment and goals
- ❏ Draft time line
- ❏ Draft statement of purpose
- ❏ Design "job" descriptions for process owner, participants, advisory group members

PRE

- ❏ Organize and schedule advisory group meetings
- ❏ Create work plan for advisory group meetings
- ❏ Distribute draft content (need, purpose)
- ❏ Distribute draft content (job descriptions, budget, time lines, and so on)
- ❏ Identify approvals needed for documentation (examples: disclaimers, agreements) and schedule reviews
- ❏ Distribute background reading from research and best practices
- ❏ Draft "plans" such as marketing plan, communication plan

❏ Design, vet, and implement mentor and mentee application and selection process (vet applications; assess candidates; select, match, and train participants)

❏ Determine budget with advisory group

❏ Design curriculum (draft, assess, and so on)

❏ Design and time line trainings

❏ Approve draft content

❏ Choose communication modes and methods from finalized plan

❏ Implement communication plan regarding mentors, mentees

❏ Schedule trainings for modes and methods

❏ Monitor budget

❏ Finalize and distribute program documents

DURING

❏ Continue advisory group meetings and post minutes

❏ Evaluate progress on work plan for advisory group meetings

❏ Maintain background reading from research and best practices

❏ Maintain content (need, purpose)

❏ Distribute final content (job descriptions, budget, time lines, and so on)

❏ Monitor communication modes and methods

❏ Monitor training for modes and methods

❏ Monitor progress of mentor/mentee relationships

❏ Gather goals, project ideas, and so on

❏ Monitor curriculum

❏ Monitor trainings

❏ Gather data and conduct evaluations of process to date, including feedback from participants, forms completed, data gathered, and so on

POST

❏ Aggregate evaluative data

❏ Assess data

❏ Work with advisory group to vet data and evaluation

❏ Consider—as appropriate—an external evaluator
❏ Audit budget
❏ Assess goal completion and success of outcomes
❏ Assess budget for economy and return on investment
❏ Identify successes, failures of communication and marketing plans
❏ Conduct assessment of the advisory group
❏ Prepare, distribute program report

## Mentor Activities Checklist

The following is a list of suggested mentor activities. Following goals and outcomes design, the pair will design a time line (example: first meeting, first month, first three months).

| # | FIRST MONTH | PROPOSED DATE | COMPLETED |
|---|---|---|---|
| 1 | Complete all application paperwork | | |
| 2 | Revise—as appropriate—work schedule with supervisor | | |
| 3 | Review background content on mentoring | | |
| 4 | Review background content on the organization's program vision, mission, and so on | | |
| 5 | Review the mentee's application and any additional profile information available | | |
| 6 | Meet with mentee to get acquainted and discuss the program overall, and discuss desired goals, outcomes, and time lines | | |
| 7 | Decide on communication preferences and schedule in any training on platform software, and so on | | |
| 8 | Review documentation required for measurement and evaluation | | |
| 9 | Identify first (period of time) activities such as trainings, tours, meetings, and so on | | |
| 10 | Outline project directions and initial time lines | | |

*(continued)*

| # | FIRST MONTH | PROPOSED DATE | COMPLETED |
|---|---|---|---|
| 11 | Finalize goals and outcomes (using approval process) and insert progress on those into time line | | |
| 12 | Identify categories and organizations of interest for professional opportunities for the mentee | | |
| 13 | Attend mentor activities as instructed | | |

# Mentee Activities Checklist

The following is a list of suggested mentee activities. Following goals and outcomes design, the pair will design a time line (example: first meeting, first month, first three months).

| # | FIRST MONTH | PROPOSED DATE | COMPLETED |
|---|---|---|---|
| 1 | Complete all application paperwork | | |
| 2 | Revise—as appropriate—work schedule with supervisor | | |
| 3 | Review background content on mentoring; roles and responsibilities of a mentee | | |
| 4 | Review background content on the organization's program vision, mission, and so on | | |
| 5 | Review the mentor's application and any additional profile information available | | |
| 6 | Draft desired goals, outcomes, and time lines | | |
| 7 | Meet with mentor to get acquainted and discuss the program overall, and discuss desired goals, outcomes, and time lines | | |
| 8 | Decide on communication preferences and schedule in any training on platform software, and so on | | |
| 9 | Review documentation required for measurement and evaluation | | |
| 10 | Identify first (period of time) activities such as trainings, tours, meetings, and so on | | |

| # | FIRST MONTH | PROPOSED DATE | COMPLETED |
|---|---|---|---|
| 11 | Update calendar to be able to outline project directions and initial time lines | | |
| 12 | Finalize goals and outcomes (using approval process) and insert progress on those into time line | | |
| 13 | Identify categories and organizations of interest for professional opportunities to share with the mentor | | |
| 14 | Attend mentee activities as instructed | | |

# CORRESPONDENCE

## Mentors

### MENTOR NOMINATION/REQUEST LETTER

Congratulations!

You have been nominated to serve as a mentor in the [name of] Mentorship Program. Annually, approximately ten employees are nominated but only five are needed, so please consider this both an honor *and* a competitive process.

Following your initial nomination, we ask for a completed application to be submitted within two weeks of your receipt of this letter. This can be submitted online through the link below and although we require people to complete the form, you are able to attach documents. Please note: a completed form; however, is needed to begin the process so only attaching a résumé will not move you to the next step.

### THE PROGRAM

As you know, the [Library/association/consortia] established a mentorship program to assist in the integration of new professionals into the [institution]. This program was established two years ago, in [location], based on a review of the past ten years of performance evaluations of new employees and an HR research project that included an assessment of the first-year professional development opportunities. It was determined, based on an Ad Hoc Task Force review, that although new professionals received a solid orientation to the organization, they did NOT receive the ongoing support identified as critical to first-year success. A subsequent organizational culture survey provided us with data that included lower levels of satisfaction from new professionals (less than two years), and our design of the mentorship program was in response to this information.

## MENTOR STATUS/BENEFITS

If you become a mentor—beyond the service to the organization, the satisfaction from assisting in the professional growth of a colleague, and the personal rejuvenation most mentors get from the process—the organizational benefits include five hours per week support from an administrative assistant to support any paperwork; unique training in and use of the Mentor Project software purchased to create a digital landscape for the relationship and the relationship project; a (monthly, annual, one-time) stipend; an additional [amount] for professional development opportunities for two years; and an automatic ten hours of required professional development credit. In addition, we inform your supervisor that—if chosen—we encourage managers to arrange for at least one full day off the reference desk and away from [classroom Information Literacy instruction] to ensure the mentor/mentee relationship has time for meeting and discussion.

As a mentor, you are required to attend three meetings the first year, use the mentorship [wiki, software, blog, and so on] at least weekly in the first three months and following as appropriate, and set an ongoing, standard schedule for communication with your mentee. Please see the *Handbook* link below for specific content and expectations as well as suggested time lines. A variety of evaluation opportunities are also required as well as general feedback opportunities. The Handbook also links you to an online pathfinder with mentoring content to review as well as links to podcasts to both past mentors and mentees.

I am hopeful you will consider this important role and join the mentor program and mentor cohort for the [20xx] year. If you have any questions, please feel free to contact me.

Sincerely,

[name]

cc: Mentor Program Advisor

Applicant's [Supervisor]

# Mentee

MENTEE NOTIFICATION LETTER

Dear [name],

We are a match! I am very pleased and honored to tell you that I have been assigned to you as your first-year mentor. Although your primary supervisor is still [name], mentors are available to first orient and then guide you through your [first year, first six months, orientation to your new department and so on] at work. We hope that this will help you make a smooth and successful transition to your [position, new roles and responsibilities, first professional job and so on] here at [location]. I have served as a mentor before, but each mentor and mentee is different so we have a clean slate.

We have our first "meet and greet" next Friday after work; however, it's a large group and it might be difficult to talk. Therefore, to get some of the "getting to know you" out of the way, please see my attached application form and profile. In addition, please visit the mentoring online guide. I will be exploring it as well before Friday, so I will have an idea of our time line!

I am very much looking forward to working with you!

Sincerely,

[name]

Mentor

[name of] Mentorship Programs

# APPLICATION FORMS

## Mentor

MENTOR APPLICATION

Thank you for applying for this important initiative. Please e-mail this completed form to [name] or mail a completed application to [name] no later than [date]. Application information will be used to select mentors and to match mentors with mentees. Forms are shared among potential mentees in the process of matching.

Name: _____

Place of Employment/Department/Location:

_____

Position Title:

_____

Circle One:  Full-time; Part-time; New Member,
              Seeking Employment; Retired (and so on)

Work Address (if applicable):

_____

City _____ State _____ Zip Code _____

Work Phone _____ Cell Phone _____

E-mail address (primary contact)_____
(If mentors/mentees use the organization's e-mail software, participants will be asked to obtain a [Gmail] address.)

What three things should we know about you to match you with a mentee? Work experience? Knowledge of a particular size or type of library? Leadership experience? Past mentoring/mentee experience?

1. _____
   _____

2. _____
   _____

3. _____
   _____

Please select no more than five areas of the profession in which you have expertise and/or experience that you would be willing to share with a mentee. Feel free to provide examples under the categories chosen such as Technical Services, Cataloging, Acquisitions, or Age-Level Services: Seniors, Youth, Young Adult, Pre-K.

| | | |
|---|---|---|
| ❏ Type of Library | ❏ Digital Librarianship | ❏ Instructional Design |
| ❏ Age-Level Services | ❏ Management | ❏ Training |
| ❏ Scholarly Communication | ❏ Supervision | ❏ Communication |
| ❏ Collection Management | ❏ Reference | ❏ Public Speaking |
| ❏ Technology (hardware) | ❏ Circulation/Access | ❏ Information Literacy |
| ❏ Technology (software) | ❏ Technology Support | ❏ Technical Services |
| ❏ Archives | ❏ Preservation | ❏ Research |
| ❏ Publication | ❏ Metadata | ❏ Other |

Degrees obtained or in progress (Degree, Institution, Location, and Graduation Date Expected):

Mentorship preferences such as "I would like to mentor:"
   ❏ female   ❏ male   ❏ no preference

Please list any non-library areas of expertise and leisure/personal interests you could share with a mentee appropriate to the workplace (example: public speaking):

_____
_____
_____

Have you ever been ☐ a mentor?   ☐ a mentee?
(Check all that apply) Please list the program if the relationship was a formal program.

Have you ever had training such as mentorship training? Leadership training?

LANGUAGES

Speak _____ Read _____ Understand _____

COMMITMENT

I understand that acceptance into the [name of] Mentorship Program as a mentor obligates me to all of the following:

- Attendance at all training activities
- Attendance at cohort discussion sessions
- Commitment to a (six month, one-year, and so on) active program and a (six month, one-year, and so on) follow-up program with my mentee
- Commitment to the communication plan agreed upon within the mentor/mentee agreement
- Commitment to the record-keeping and evaluation of the relationship
- Abiding by the confidentiality guidelines of the mentor/mentee program

Mentor Applicant Signature _____

Date _____

If applicable, supervisor initials _____

# Mentee

## MENTEE APPLICATION

Thank you for applying for this important initiative. Please e-mail this completed form to [name] or mail a completed application to [name] no later than [date]. Application information will be used to select mentees and to match mentees with mentors. Forms are shared among potential mentors in the process of matching.

Name: _____

Place of Employment/Department/Location

_____

Position Title: _____

Circle One:  Full-time; Part-time; New Member;
            Seeking Employment; Intern (and so on)

Work Address (if applicable):

_____

City _____ State _____ Zip Code_____

Work Phone_____ Cell Phone _____

E-mail address (primary contact)_____
(If mentors/mentees use the organization's e-mail software, participants will be asked to obtain a [Gmail] address.)

What three things should we know about you to match you with a mentor? Education? Work experience? Desire of knowledge of a particular size or type of library and leadership experience? Desire of specific networking opportunities? Desire for a specific skill or ability?

1. _____
   _____

2. _____
   _____

3. _____
   _____

What are your reasons—in general—for wanting a mentor? (Check all that apply)

- ❏ Networking (within the organization; the profession)
- ❏ Experience with unique competencies (noted elsewhere on the application)
- ❏ Direction/guidance for my career/general career development
- ❏ Orientation to the institution or organization
- ❏ Assistance with first-year organization requirements
- ❏ Introduction to professional association membership and service
- ❏ Direction and guidance on work issues (access to or assistance from someone other than my supervisor as appropriate)

What are no more than two areas of the profession in which you have an interest or desire to learn about with or from a mentor? Feel free to be more specific by adding examples under the categories chosen such as Technical Services, Cataloging, Acquisitions, or Age-Level Services: Seniors, Youth, Young Adult, Pre-K.

| | | |
|---|---|---|
| ❏ Type of Library | ❏ Digital Librarianship | ❏ Instructional Design |
| ❏ Age-Level Services | ❏ Management | ❏ Training |
| ❏ Scholarly Communication | ❏ Supervision | ❏ Communication |
| ❏ Collection Management | ❏ Reference | ❏ Public Speaking |
| ❏ Technology (hardware) | ❏ Circulation/Access | ❏ Information Literacy |
| ❏ Technology (software) | ❏ Technology Support | ❏ Technical Services |
| ❏ Archives | ❏ Preservation | ❏ Research |
| ❏ Publication | ❏ Metadata | ❏ Other |

Degrees obtained/in progress (Degree, Institution, Location, Graduation Date, or Expected):

Mentee preferences such as "I would like to be mentored by:"
❑ female   ❑ male   ❑ no preference

Please list any non-library areas of expertise and leisure or personal interests appropriate to the workplace that you feel would enrich the mentor/mentee experience (example: public speaking):

_____

Have you ever been ❑ a mentor? ❑ a mentee? (Check all that apply) Please list the program if the relationship was a formal program.

Have you ever had training such as mentor or mentee training? Leadership training?

LANGUAGES:

Speak _____ Read _____ Understand _____

COMMITMENT

I understand that acceptance into the [name] Mentorship Program as a mentee obligates me to all of the following:

- Attendance at all training activities
- Attendance at cohort discussion sessions
- Commitment to a one-year active program and a one-year follow-up program with my mentee
- Commitment to the communication plan agreed upon within the mentor/mentee agreement
- Commitment to the record-keeping and evaluation of the relationship
- Abiding by the confidentiality guidelines of the mentor/mentee program

Mentee Applicant Signature _____

Date _____

If applicable, supervisor initials _____

# RECOMMENDATION FORMS

## Applicant Recommendation Form

You have been identified as someone who will provide a recommendation for an applicant for the [name of] Mentorship Program. Please complete this form in support of the application and if you feel you cannot recommend this applicant, please return the form with the appropriate box checked.

Applicant _____

Application is submitted in pursuit of

Mentor _____

Mentee _____

❑ I am able to recommend the applicant.

❑ I am not able to recommend the applicant.

**1.** My relationship to the applicant is: _____

**2.** The applicant is a good candidate for the Mentorship Program because: _____

**3.** This applicant brings two strengths to the program:

_____

**4.** This applicant should be chosen over other candidates because:

_____

**5.** The best match for this applicant would be someone who:

_____

# EVALUATION CONTENT

Although evaluation forms must match the program goals and outcomes, examples of evaluative questions include:

- ❏ My mentor possessed the content expertise in my area of need.
- ❏ My mentor demonstrated content expertise in my area of need.
- ❏ My mentor was available and approachable.
- ❏ My mentor was supportive of my work and when addressing other questions and concerns.
- ❏ My mentor provided the feedback necessary for me to complete my project successfully.
- ❏ My mentor's feedback was constructive and useful.
- ❏ My mentor motivated me to complete my mentee activities.
- ❏ My mentor assisted me in identifying appropriate networking opportunities and assisted me in connecting with those networks.
- ❏ My mentor adhered to communication plan time lines.
- ❏ My mentor suggested appropriate resources in a timely manner.

Additional elements to evaluate with annotated Likert scale responses include the following statements. The statements are deliberately not consistent in order to provide variety and choice.

1. As a result of the pairing, I experienced a rejuvenation in my profession.  ❏ Yes  ❏ No

2. I have increased satisfaction with my job.  ❏ Yes  ❏ No

3. I was pleased with my pairing/match.  ❏ Yes  ❏ No

4. I observed overall satisfaction with other relationship pairings. ❑ Yes ❑ No

5. What role(s) did your mentor assume in this relationship and did they contribute to the success of the match? Check all that apply.

   a. ❑ Teacher
      ❑ Counselor
      ❑ Advisor
      ❑ Sponsor
      ❑ Research Guide

   b. ❑ Advocate
      ❑ Resource
      ❑ Other (explain below)

6. Did the communication modes and methods agreed upon work for you? If not, please give two reasons why they didn't and—if you have an opinion or knowledge of other, better modes and methods—please suggest alternatives.

   _____

7. Please list two reasons you feel your relationship is/was a success?

   _____

8. Please list two strengths and two weaknesses of your mentor/ mentee relationship.

   _____

9. I have more confidence in my work environment since I completed the Mentoring Program because:

   _____

# BIBLIOGRAPHY AND RESOURCES

**B**IBLIOGRAPHIES ARE DESIGNED to document sources used as background in writing and research. While a wide variety of sources can be used to expand subject content for the author, a number of resources are also highly recommended for readers to use in expanding their knowledge beyond this book *and* for designing their own mentorship program. Therefore, this bibliography is divided into two sections.

- *Section 1* includes those resources to be used in the process of expanding knowledge for solid context and background reading. Each source contributes to the overall topic by providing a bigger picture of the importance of mentorship programs or through illustrating unique, focused content. Resources in section 1 are not annotated.
- *Section 2* includes those resources to be used in the process of expanding knowledge with recommendations for use in the course of deciding whether or not an organization will have a program at all; the type of program such as formal or informal, pilot or permanent; in the course of building the program chosen; and, for unique program needs given the type and size of organization or setting or unique needs of the organization, the mentor pool, the mentee pool, or participant goals. Resources in section 2 are annotated.

In addition, the resources included in both sections include materials from library and information science, other disciplines or areas, print and online sources, classic and contemporary or new. The resources are a mix of articles, monographs, research, and websites. In addition, there are sources with a mix of content including all types of writing and content presentation; narrative or description; technical writing; forms and templates; and—of course—research, reporting, and opinion.

## Section 1

Bloomquist, Catherine. "Mentoring Gen-X Librarians." *Public Libraries Online.* May/June 2014. http://publiclibrariesonline.org/2014/07/mentoring-gen-x-librarians.

DeZelar-Tiedman, Christine, Beth Picknally Camden, and Rebecca Uhl. "Growing Our Own: Mentoring the Next Generation of Catalog Librarians." *Cataloging & Classification Quarterly* 43 (2006): 19–35.

Eby, Lillian, Marcus Butts, Angie Lockwood, and Shana A. Simon. "Protégés' Negative Mentoring Experiences." *Personnel Psychology* 57, no. 2 (2004): 411–47.

Ensher, Ellen A., and Susan E. Murphy. *Power Mentoring: How Successful Mentors and Protégés Get the Most Out of Their Relationships.* 1st ed. San Francisco: Jossey-Bass, 2005.

Keener, Molly, Vicki Johnson, and Bobbie L. Collins. "In-House Collaborative Mentoring." *College & Research Libraries News,* 73 no. 3 (March 2012): 134–46.

Kochan, Frances K., and Joseph T. Pascarelli. *Global Perspectives on Mentoring: Transforming Contexts, Communities, and Cultures.* Charlotte, NC: Information Age Publishing, 2003. http://books.google.com/books/about/Global_Perspectives_on_Mentoring.html?id=En0wc4bwyfIC.

Kuyper-Rushing, L. "A Formal Mentoring Program in a University Library: Components of a Successful Experiment." *The Journal of Academic Librarianship* 27 no. 6 (2001): 440–46.

Level, Allison V. and Michelle Mach. "Peer Mentoring: One Institution's Approach to Mentoring Academic Librarians." *Library Management* 26, no. 6/7 (2005): 301–10.

Metz, Ruth F. *Coaching in the Library: A Management Strategy for Achieving Excellence.* 2nd ed. Chicago: American Library Association, 2011.

Munde, Gail. "Beyond Mentoring: Toward the Rejuvenation of Academic Libraries." *Journal of Academic Librarianship,* 26, no. 3 (May 2000): 171–75.

Portner, Hal. *Being Mentored: A Guide for Protégés.* Thousand Oaks: Corwin, 2011.

Wicks, Robert J. *Sharing Wisdom: The Practical Art of Giving and Receiving Mentoring.* New York: Crossroad, 2000.

# Section 2

## American Library Association. www.ala.org.

The American Library Association, as the premier international library and information science professional association, is the primary environment to find content on mentoring. Organizations or individuals with goals including individual career success, overall career development, and organizational growth and enhancement as well as recruitment to the profession and professional organizations can find both general mentoring content as well as programs for functional areas of the profession. ALA's significant web environment offers both members and guests content through a variety of modes and methods including general content (in print and media) from conference programming, narrative explanation, research and reporting; pathfinders and bibliographies; opinions and testimonials; and examples of forms and templates used for existing mentoring activities. While not all content is accessible to guests or visitors, a significant amount of mentor content *is* available on the ALA's website. Examples of ALA content accessible to guests can be found at (but not limited to) "ALA Mentoring & Recruitment Efforts": www.ala.org/educationcareers/mentoring/mentoring_and_recruitment_efforts.

### *General ALA Examples*

- ALA's Connect is a member hybrid program (with both digital and in-person opportunities) and is available through the Association's web-based software "Connect." Although the software is not available to guests or visitors, there is an excellent general association FAQ that could be used as a model by associations and organizations to describe the use of the mode to create digital partnerships. Connect is found at www.connect.ala.org/mentorconnect-help. All types and sizes of libraries and all types of librarians may apply to participate.
- ALA's Emerging Leaders longer-term initiatives include mentor and mentee training and matching for career development both during conferences and throughout professionals' work lives. http://wikis.ala.org/emergingleaders/index.php/Main_Page. All types and sizes of libraries and all types of librarians may apply to participate.
- ALA's Office of Human Resource Development and Recruitment supports all types and sizes of libraries in career development activities. An extensive bibliography, "Library Leadership Training Resources," offers links to over twenty leadership programs with affiliate and non-affiliate groups—many of which use mentorship aspects to both deliver and supplement curriculum. www.ala.org/offices/hrdr and www.ala.org/offices/hrdr/abouthrdr/hrdrliaisoncomm/otld/leadershiptraining.
- ALA's Spectrum Scholarship Program emanates from ALA's Office for Diversity and is primarily a recruitment-to-the-profession through graduate education for diverse individuals such as people of color. There are informal and formal mentoring aspects to Spectrum participants both during their educational programs and post-graduate education through

some university master's programs as well as through some initiatives in ALA groups such as ACRL. www.ala.org/offices/diversity/spectrum.

## ALA Roundtable Examples

- ALA's New Member's Roundtable (NMRT) "business" is that of mentoring. To this end, NMRT offers hybrid opportunities that include digital connections with an ALA member assigned to a mentee for general online pairings for professional support, semi-monthly discussion opportunities, and designated monthly discussion topics. While program goals include networking, advice, and guidance as well as increased confidence for newcomers to the profession and newcomers to ALA, NMRT identifies their goal as "Career Mentoring" and supports the overall process with other services such as résumé review and other conference activities. All types and sizes of libraries and all types of librarians may apply to participate. www.ala.org/nmrt/initiatives/nmrtmentguide/nmrtmentoring and www.ala.org/ala/mgrps/rts/nmrt/oversightgroups/comm/mentor/conference MentorApp.cfm.

- Several ALA Roundtable programs exist in various stages of activity designed to meet both shorter and longer-term needs. These include (but are not limited to) the International Relations Roundtable (IRRT), International Librarians' Orientation/Mentoring Committee (www.ala.org/irrt/irrt-international-librarians-orientationmentoring-committee). There are also shorter-term initiatives for ALA Annual Conference matches and Midwinter activities for welcoming and orienting international visitors. An ALA "one-shot" mentor or "buddy" program example is the Gay, Lesbian, Bisexual, and Transgender Round Table (GLBTRT) Buddy Program (www.ala.org/glbtrt/involved/buddy). Designed to pair new or returning ALA members for introductions to association conference activities and round table members, the program offers people short-term mentoring for ALA in general and Roundtable initiatives. A valuable addition to the idea of association mentoring initiatives is the inclusion of a category of individual who is interested in mentoring and is returning to the association after a long absence. All types and sizes of libraries and all types of librarians may apply to participate.

## ALA Division Examples

### ACRL

The Association of College and Research Libraries (ACRL) offers extensive, varied mentoring opportunities throughout the division to meet membership needs. They include relationships in the focused areas of type and/or size of library, management, research and promotion, expanded representation of diversity, teaching and learning and discipline-specific growth. Website content includes research, articles, best practices, and—for example—best practices conference content. The ACRL's sections include:

- ACRL College Libraries Section (CLS)—The College Library Directors Mentor Program (www.acrl.org/ala/mgrps/divs/acrl/

about/sections/cls/collprogdisc/collegelibrary.cfm) is a twenty-year program that pairs experienced college library directors with a new-to-management librarian at a college or for first-year-at-a-college library director. An extensive FAQ on the section's ACRL site offers in-depth content to interested applicants and the program has an associated cost for initial orientation and training.

- ACRL College Libraries Section—The "Your Research Coach Program" exists to provide expertise to librarians involved in research and scholarly writing for publication and tenure. Mentors and mentees or "research coaches" and "research partners" have a wide selection of activities for the primarily digital relationship. www.ala.org/acrl/aboutacrl/directoryofleadership/sections/cls/clswebsite/collprogdisc/researchcoach.

- ACRL's Dr. E. J. Josey Mentoring Program for Spectrum Scholars—This ACRL mentoring program exists to support the ALA Spectrum Program initiative for Spectrum Scholar participants committed to academic librarianship. The program matches Spectrum library school students and/or newly graduated librarians with experienced academic librarians for career development in academic libraries. www.ala.org/acrl/membership/mentoring/joseymentoring/mentorprogram.

- ACRL Instruction Section (IS) Mentoring Program—This ACRL/IS Mentoring Program focuses on developing academic librarians new to the Instruction Section or new to teaching and learning and information literacy (IL) instruction. Through this program, expert IL librarians are matched with librarians seeking growth in instruction skills. The IS program web page provides links to forms and tip sheets and a link to a bibliography of content on contemporary mentoring. www.ala.org/acrl/aboutacrl/directoryofleadership/sections/is/iswebsite/projpubs/mentoring

- ACRL Literatures in English Section—Although this section's hybrid (in-person and digital) mentor program has simple forms and processes, the premise is unique in that the section wishes to recruit, nurture, and support existing and potential humanities subject-specialist librarians. Experienced humanities librarian matches are available for work-related problem-solving and other work challenges, networking with other humanities and related subject-specialist professionals, and support and networking at ALA conferences. www.ala.org/acrl/aboutacrl/directoryofleadership/sections/lesmentors.

- ACRL Science & Technology Section (STS): Sci/Tech Library Mentors Find a Mentor—The STS Section's mentoring goal is broad and offers opportunities to find a mentor if a librarian has a large or small library-related issue that needs solving. Both for academic and special career focuses, STS's program is hybrid and includes all modes and methods of discussion for any timelines desired. www.ala.org/acrl/aboutacrl/directoryofleadership/sections/sts/stswebsite/mentors/findmentor.

● Besides mentor programs available throughout the Division, ACRL offers a Chapter's Council for state ACRL chapter leaders with an orientation handbook and mentor ideas for chapter member engagement. Besides the manual, an ACRL Chapter's Blog serves as an information-sharing forum that includes mentoring activities at state levels. Many ACRL state chapters offer mentorship program opportunities, including Maryland, Delaware, Pennsylvania, Georgia, California, and Louisiana—to name only a few. www.ala.org/acrl/sites/ala.org.acrl/files/content/ACRL%20Chapters%20Orientation%20Toolkit%20January%202014_1.pdf.

## AASL

The American Association of School Librarians (AASL) has extensive content on mentoring school librarians, which is especially important in solo librarian environments, including a seventy-page Mentor/Mentee Collaborating Partners Handbook, with program rubrics, membership survey and survey results, conference programming content in print and media, and more than a dozen 30 Second Thought Leadership podcasts. http://aasl.ala.org/essentiallinks/index.php?title=mentoring.

## ALCTS

ALA's Association of Library Collections and Technical Services Cataloging & Metadata Management Section (CaMMS) Recruitment & Mentoring Committee (ALCTS) allows all ALA members to participate in the mentorship program and also advertises for specific types of libraries, specific expertise from mentors and specific types of librarians such as new and practicing catalog librarians and graduate students interested in cataloging. Mentorship projects include discussions on graduate-level cataloging coursework, continuing education for catalogers, and career development such as résumé design, and review and interviewing techniques. www.ala.org/alcts/mgrps/camms/cmtes/ats-ccsrecment.

## ALSC

A variety of mentoring opportunities has long been available through ALA's Association for Library Service to Children (ALSC). A 2014 division-wide revamping of the ALSC mentor program, however, offers multiple program and relationship goals, expanded discussion topics, hybrid activities, a Mentoring Forum, and expanded online resources with bibliographies and blog postings. Additional changes to mentoring opportunities include expanded goals such as new and early career librarian skill building, expanded awareness of children's librarians competencies, encouraging and providing opportunities for networking, sharing peer expertise, reinvigorating mid-to-end career professionals, the role of association service as a cornerstone of the profession, and leadership development for recruiting and training ALSC leaders. www.ala.org/alsc/mentoring

## LLAMA

ALA's Library Leadership and Management Association (LLAMA) offers significant mentor content digitally and in print. The division's web environment includes the values of mentoring, mentor program goals, forms, templates, and program tips as well as an orientation video stream found through the division's Mentoring Committee www.ala.org/ala/mgrps/divs/llama/committees/LLAMA_Mentoring_Committee/LLAMA_Mentor_Application.pdf. The online program includes a Mentor Program Guide (www.ala.org/llama/committees/mentoring/LLAMA_Formal_Mentoring_GuideMentan) application form, and a mentor fact sheet. www.ala.org/ala/mgrps/divs/llama/committees/LLAMA_Mentoring_Committee/Mentor_Fact_Sheet.pdf.

## PLA

ALA's Public Library Association (PLA) web environment includes a number of references to mentorship; however, the majority of resources, programs, and initiatives are under "Leadership Development" or in the goals statement or statement of benefits for the PLA "Leadership Academy." www.ala.org/pla/leadership and www.ala.org/pla/education/leadershipacademy.

## YALSA

ALA's Young Adult Library Association (YALSA). YALSA's virtual mentoring program matches experienced librarians with new librarians or graduate students in library programs. The program strongly encourages practicing librarians with roles and responsibilities in programming, collection development, and reader's advisory to create relationship goals and connect virtually and monthly (and face-to-face as possible and desired) and to collaborate on a project to be completed during the internship year. Monthly activities include discussion topics and a resource list for review and reflection. Although participants (identified as mentors and protégés) will choose virtual modes and methods for meeting, the division provides space on ALA Connect. Additional program infrastructure includes quarterly training sessions and a final evaluation. www.ala.org/yalsa/profdev/mentoring.

## ALA/APA

ALA's Allied Professionals Association (APA) offers conference programming on human resources issues—including mentoring—and *Library Worklife: HR ENews for Today's Leaders*. The *ALA/APA Newsletter* provides not only articles but news content on human resources issues affecting mentoring roles and responsibilities in organizations. *The Library Worklife* website not only has frequent and current postings, but provides all newsletter content for free and full text in the website with a search function and an index. Additional mentoring-related content is available in leadership and networking content. http://ala-apa.org.

*All About Mentoring.* New York: SUNY Empire State College, 2014. http://media.esc.edu/2014/aam-summer/HTML/index.html#2/z.

Since 2011, editor Alan Mandell's online journal *All About Mentoring* has provided significant content in the field of mentoring. Program designers as well as mentors and mentees should acquaint themselves with this journal if for no other reason than to learn about the breadth of mentorship, including scholarly research, opinions and ideas about adult learning, teaching and mentoring, and best practices.

### American Society for Training and Development (ASTD). www.astd.org.

ASTD is one of the premier websites for training and development and online offerings include free and fee-based content. Searching ASTD for "mentorship" yields dozens of articles and posts for organizations wishing to design mentor programs, mentors looking for training, and mentees looking for mentor programs.

### American Society of Association Executives (ASAE). *The Center for Association Leadership.* www.asaecenter.org.

Searching ASAE's *Center* website yields over 700 results for "mentor," and although not all of these links are free or applicable to library mentoring initiatives, extensive content is available on mentoring, mentors and mentees, as well as basic program design. In addition, *Associations Now*'s current and archived full-text content includes extensive, valuable, contemporary, and very relevant mentor content on topics such as mentoring millennials, the career value of mentoring in associations, and best practice programs.

### Arizona State University Libraries. *Academic Personnel: Online Resources for Mentoring.* https://provost.asu.edu/academic_personnel/mentoring.

ASU's Library web environment is an extensive pathfinder designed to support the overall university's mentorship programs and opportunities. The website should be viewed for the design and coordination of extensive links culled from best practices as well as original content that articulates the university's various programs. Besides ASU's initiatives, basic and advanced content on mentoring is available for designers to use as a model for organizing mentor content.

### Association of Research Libraries (ARL). *SPEC Kits: Overview.*

Over 200 SPEC kits are available for purchase (online or in print) or interlibrary loan. Classic mentor content can be found in Barbara Wittkopf's *Mentoring Programs in ARL Libraries,* SPEC Kit 239, as well as in more current content from a number of kits that focus on leadership and the training and orientation of academic librarians. In addition, much of the content is helpful to different types and sizes of libraries. http://publications.arl.org/SPEC_Kits. Additional resources are available through ARL's "Digital Publications," including online articles. http://publications.arl.org/title_index.

### "Big Dog's & Little Dog's Performance Juxtaposition." http://nwlink .com/~donclark.

Big Dog's site—an extensive collection of content for leadership—among many other content areas provides dozens of links to content on mentoring for today's organization, including extensive information for nonprofits. Website content is designed as an FAQ and initial information is synthesized on each page; however, those interested in broader information or more in-depth specifics should note suggested free e-books and white papers as well as links to other content. Big Dog also offers templates and forms for mentorship program design, and those designing programs will find a number of for-profit and for-sale content; however, free content is extensive. In addition, a newer focus for content includes "Mentoring with Social Media," which illustrates how mentors connect with mentees not only through social media or web-based forums, but also general virtual and digital mentoring ideas. www.nw link.com/~donclark/leader/mentor/mentoring_social_media.html.

Bell, Steven. "The Next Generation May Not Want Your Mentoring." *Leading from the Library. Library Journal.* April 24, 2013. http://lj.libraryjournal .com/2013/04/opinion/leading-from-the-library/the-next-generation-may -not-want-your-mentoring-leading-from-the-library/#_.

Always thought-provoking, Bell's article offers much to consider in planning mentor programs and mentorship opportunities for all librarians today and especially those newer to the field. While he offers warnings on curriculum, approach, and delivery, he continues to fully support mentoring in libraries, but provides valuable recommendations on where programs need to change.

Brazil Leadership Program. "Mentoring." https://www.andrews.edu/sed/lead ership_dept/documents/mentoring_competency.pdf.

Although much work goes into mentorship program design, an equal amount of work needs to go into designing a curriculum for both mentors and mentees illustrating the teaching and learning roles and responsibilities and techniques for imparting knowledge through the relationship. This short article provides an overview of the understanding needed for the establishment of the stages of the relationship and the theory behind adult learning in a mentoring relationship.

EDUCAUSE. www.educause.edu.

EDUCAUSE provides extensive online content for mentoring. Although—in general—the content is geared to Primary through Higher Education or P–16 educational settings, the vast majority of both original and linked content is applicable in some way or another to all types and sizes of libraries. Although EDUCAUSE also offers many publications for sale, extensive content is available online, including an information kit (www.educause.edu/mentoring), content under "career planning," and specific guidance for the mentee (or protégé). Additional content is available under "learning collaborations" and "professional development."

Free Management Library. www.freemanagementlibrary.org.

This online environment offers significant content on mentoring in general as well as program descriptions, research, and forms and templates. Mentorship program designers will find explanatory content useful, but there are also links to even more helpful examples and best practices. While searching "mentoring" yields over 600 entries, and some of those links appear to work intermittently, overall, the recommended content is valuable for additional links to web environments such as *Chief Learning Officer* with additional extensive and helpful information on contemporary mentoring in organizations.

Gibson, Rita. "Mentoring and Libraries: A Bibliography." *COLT Council on Library/Media Technicians.* 2003. http://colt.ucr.edu/bibmentoring.html.

More than 100 works are included in this older but classic list of general and support staff mentoring resources. Ranging from the 1980s to 2003, the majority of sources are citations to print materials and—although the web links are very few and several aren't working—over 90 resources provide a rich foundation of mentoring materials for library mentorship program planners.

Hansman, Catherine A., ed. *Critical Perspectives on Mentoring: Trends and Issues Information Series 388.* Columbus, Ohio: ERIC Clearinghouse on Adult, Career, and Vocational Education Center on Education and Training for Employment, 2002. http://calpro-online.org/eric/docs/mott/mentoring1.pdf.

Hansman offers significant content on mentoring research to support the design of effective mentoring programs. Two specific chapters on "Telementoring" and "Diversity and Power in Mentoring Relationships" provide unique insight into twenty-first-century mentorship programs and should drive the design of aspects of contemporary programs. Although taking the longer ten-years-later look at "telementoring" yields a different terminology for "e-mentoring," this content is very relevant for considering infrastructure and mentor/mentee behaviors.

*InfoPeople: Helping Libraries Think Differently.* California State Library. http://infopeople.org.

The InfoPeople web environment provides content and training to those who work in academic, public, school, or special California libraries. Although the primary users are California librarians and library workers, others can use past training materials as well as view specific webinars and podcasts for free. Although there is much content on library-specific functions such as programming, services, and collections, a search of "mentoring" yields dozens of links with forms, templates, and examples.

Lee, Marta K. *Mentoring in the Library: Building for the Future.* Chicago: American Library Association, 2011.

Lee's book is a must-read for mentoring program designers with specific content on the benefits of mentoring for recruitment to the profession as well as benefits for the organization. Lee also covers skill sets needed by mentors and mentees, the differences between formal and informal arrangements, and a chapter on electronic modes and methods for mentoring.

**Libguides Community. www.libguides.com.**

Searching the 400,000+ Libguides in the Libguides Community and including all types of libraries in the search for "mentoring" provides dozens of guides with many elements of mentoring, including specific mentor programs in (primarily academic) institutions and general mentoring content, as well as mentoring initiatives throughout institutions and mentoring handbooks with structured content for mentors and mentees.

**Library of Congress. www.loc.gov.**

When researching "mentoring," the Library of Congress web environment links to vast content—much of which is *not* of interest to, for example, mentor program designers. Within the content, however, are valuable online government manuals, online full-text magazines and periodicals, as well as a variety of handbooks. Program designers may have to sort through a number of related—rather than specific—content, but there are a number of excellent resources available.

**Mentor. National Mentoring Partnership. www.mentoring.org.**

Extensive content on every aspect of mentoring is available from the National Mentoring Partnership website. Mentoring program designers should take note of research and data and online toolkits.

**Nebraska Library Commission. *21st Century Librarian Mentoring Program.* http://nowhiringatyourlibrary.ne.gov/Mentoring.asp.**

Although this program has been suspended due to lack of funding and a few links are no longer accessible, program web pages offer valuable content in simple terms. Program designers will learn from the simple design as well as from content lists of program and mentor and mentee benefits, as well as from the handbook.

**New Members Round Table (NMRT). *NMRT Mentor Program.* Texas Library Association. www.txla.org/groups/nmrt-mentor; http://txla.org/groups/NMRT-on-the-spot.**

While the NMRT web environment provides some general content on the Round Table's mentorship program as well as several forms, the real strength of the web content can be found on the "On-the-Spot Mentors." This unique, detailed NMRT project infrastructure complements the longer-term mentor program elements with an extensive list of functional areas of libraries and then an extensive list of individuals under each area who have signed on to an "on demand" mentor for answering questions from new librarians, library school students, or librarians new to an area. Over thirty categories (examples: types of libraries, technical services functions, age-level services, and collection development) have multiple on-the-spot mentors to seek out, and the chart includes names, titles, environments, and e-mail addresses. While this aspect of the committee provides support as intended, it also provides a training ground for short-term mentors to become longer-term mentors.

### Special Library Association (SLA). www.sla.org.

While SLA offers a little content from their public website on mentoring, they do offer content on their internal or membership pages. What *is* on the open web includes news, programs of interest, and conference training, while the primary special library content with general research and writing can be found on special library state chapters' websites. While this content can be found on the open web, the overall SLA site provides links—when searching "mentoring," for example—to state chapter mentoring content, and an SLA Libguide specifically for academics offers links to mentor content. http://slaacademic.libguides.com/content.php?pid=243207&sid=2505263

### Stephen's Lighthouse. http://stephenslighthouse.com.

Although this website (from the home page) is not easily able to be searched for content, a Google search of this web environment and "mentoring" language offers a number of links of commentary and opinion. Although the website is considered hosted by Stephen Abrams, the content is created through individual authorship of content, content and comments from Abrams, and comments on content from a number of people in and related to the profession.

### Webjunction. www.webjunction.org.

Webjunction has delivered content and training to librarians and libraries since 2003. The website offers both fee-based continuing education and content for all types of libraries, with over seventy-five links to mentoring content. Although a few links are no longer active, Webjunction website users can find significant handbooks, manuals, and forms and templates to assist them in mentoring program design.

### Workforce. www.workforce.com.

Workforce—primarily a tool for non-library profit and profit environments—offers mentoring resources including related news and human resources trends for mentoring. Content provided includes journal articles, news articles, case studies, scenarios, and research, and although the terminology may be different (example: onboarding instead of orientation) there is significant relevant information. Additional workplace web environments to monitor for mentoring content include HR.BLR.org: Compliance Tools for HR Professionals (http://hr.blr.com) and HRVoice.org (the website of HRMA) at www.HRVoice.org.

# INDEX